PERFORMERS

◆ ◆ ◆

AMERICAN INDIAN LIVES

PERFORMERS

◆ ◆ ◆

Liz Sonneborn

Facts On File®

AN INFOBASE HOLDINGS COMPANY

On the cover: (left) Will Rogers; (right) Maria Tallchief

Performers

Copyright © 1995 by Liz Sonneborn

Facts On File, Inc.
460 Park Avenue South
New York NY 10016

Library of Congress Cataloging-in-Publication Data

Sonneborn, Liz.
    Performers / Liz Sonneborn.
      p. cm. — (American Indian lives)
    Includes bibliographical references and index.
    ISBN 0-8160-3045-6
      1. Indians in the performing arts—North America—Biography—
Juvenile literature. 2. Indian arts—North America—Juvenile
literature. [1. Entertainers. 2. Indians of North America—
Biography.] I. Title. II. Series: American Indian lives (New
York, N.Y.)
    E89.S66 1995
    791'.089'97—dc20   94-25587
    [B]

Facts On File books are available at special discounts when purchased in bulk quantities for businesses, associations, institutions or sales promotions. Please call our Special Sales Department in New York at 212/683-2244 or 800/322-8755.

Text design by Ellen Levine
Cover design by Nora Wertz
Printed in the United States of America

MP FOF 10 9 8 7 6 5 4 3 2 1

This book is printed on acid-free paper.

CONTENTS

❖ ❖ ❖

INTRODUCTION

◆ ◆ ◆

Long before non-Indians arrived in North America, there were Indian performers—storytellers, dancers, singers, actors, and musicians. At tribal gatherings, these people were called on to entertain their friends and relatives, but they also had a greater responsibility. Through their art, they were charged with ensuring that their tribe's history was remembered and their traditions remained alive. Before contact with whites, only a few of the hundreds of North American Indian groups had a written language with which to record the events and beliefs that had shaped them as a people. Instead, they relied on performers to pass along their cultural values from generation to generation through the repetition of ancient stories and the staging of ceremonies that told these tales through song and dance.

Because of the crucial role they played in Indian societies, adept Indian performers traditionally could gain great prestige among their people. Soon after non-Indians came to a tribe's homeland, however, the importance of its performers inevitably eroded. The turmoil caused by the non-Indians' presence disrupted all aspects of Indian culture, but because of the public nature of the performing arts, they were particularly vulnerable to interference by whites. Confused by unfamiliar rituals and fearful that any gathering of Indians might lead to a violent attack, non-Indians generally did whatever they could to prevent Indians from coming together to enact their ceremonial rites.

By the middle of the 19th century, missionaries and government authorities systemized these efforts to discourage the performance of ceremonies and destroy other central elements of

Indian culture. Reasoning that, for both the good of the state and of Indians themselves, tribespeople needed to abandon their old ways, these non-Indians used schools, churches, and legislation to assimilate Indians forcibly into the mainstream culture. By the end of the century, the assimilationists had largely achieved their goals. Most Indians were then confined to reservation lands, where they were easily policed by representatives of the government. Demoralized by the loss of their land and their subsequent poverty, fewer and fewer reservation Indians persisted in practicing their tribal rituals. Those who did were routinely arrested and sometimes killed by white authorities. Yet, largely through the efforts of these cultural guardians, some Indian legends and ceremonies have endured; knowledge of many more, however, have been lost forever.

Although some of the Indian entertainers discussed in this book have drawn on the surviving arts for inspiration, overall they have relatively little in common with the anonymous native performers of long ago. The performers profiled here came of age in a different America—one in which whites outnumbered Indians, and the dominant culture was defined by European Americans. These entertainers also have had to attract a different type of audience. Traditional Indian ceremonialists had performed for their peers— other Indians who understood that their role was both to instruct and entertain. These performers have had to play to non-Indians with a wide variety of expectations. Some of their audiences have wanted to learn about another culture or just to be entertained. But others came to see these performers for less benevolent motives—ranging from wanting to mock a member of a despised race to hoping to gain status through a pose of support for an unempowered minority.

The performers themselves had a myriad of reasons for choosing a career in show business. For the first two subjects—Emily Pauline Johnson and Luther Standing Bear—money was an important incentive. Born in the late 19th century, both faced overwhelming obstacles in earning a living because of their ethnicity. In the world of entertainment, however, Johnson and Standing Bear discovered that their Indianness was an asset. By the early

20th century, when they began their performing careers, large-scale Indian military resistance to the white encroachment of their land had ended. No longer considered a threat, Indians had been popularly romanticized as "a vanishing race"—a noble, defeated people with no place in the modern world. Although from dissimilar backgrounds and social classes, the audiences of both the lowbrow Wild West show in which Standing Bear appeared and the highbrow recitals in which Johnson read poems about Indian life paid their admission in part to have a look at an Indian before the race died out. In truth, Indian peoples were not vanishing, as these non-Indians perhaps wished to believe; most Native Americans merely had been hidden away on reservation lands where few non-Indians were likely to see them or their desperate poverty.

Johnson and Standing Bear were more than eager to profit from non-Indians' curiosity, but they had their own price to pay in the bargain. To please their audiences, they sometimes had to sensationalize and otherwise distort their experiences and those of other Indian people, and, in the process, propagate damaging stereotypes that they abhorred. Despite attempts to rationalize away their discomfort, Johnson's rage at herself and her audience always bubbled beneath her veneer of composure, whereas Standing Bear's anger surfaced full-blown in the memoirs he authored late in his life.

Indianness played a substantially lesser role in the careers of Will Rogers and Maria Tallchief: for the most part, they became successful performers in spite of their Indian heritage rather than because of it. Both worked in fields far removed from any traditional native performing arts. An early star of vaudeville, Rogers became internationally famous as a film comedian in the 1930s. Tallchief was known around the globe as the world's premier ballerina in the 1950s. Their Indian ancestry was frequently noted by the press, but usually presented more as trivia than as a notable influence on their work.

The public's relative disinterest in the backgrounds of these celebrities was in keeping with popular notions of Indianness in the mid-20th century. Despite the efforts of traditionalists in many

Indian communities to follow the ways of their ancestors, Indian culture was considered extinct by most non-Indians. The U.S. government encouraged this idea in its promotion of the termination policy in the 1950s. Seeking release from its small monetary obligations to Indian groups as a result of certain 19th-century treaties, the United States tried to terminate the legal Indian status of many vibrant Indian communities by maintaining that their old traditions were meaningless in modern America.

While living Indians seemed invisible to mainstream America, their ancestors held a peculiar fascination for legions of moviegoers. Until the mid-1960s, westerns were the most popular American film genre. They often featured Indian characters and sometimes Indian actors, but they very rarely presented an Indian perspective on Western history. Tribal leaders and warriors were usually caricatured as ignoble primitives, whose battles with non-Indians were motivated sheerly by bloodlust. Lacking any familiarity with actual Indians or knowledge of Indian cultures, many Americans came to define all Indian peoples, past and present, according to this crude, but potent screen stereotype.

Actor Iron Eyes Cody, whose career in Hollywood spanned most of the 20th century, witnessed firsthand the evolution of the image of Indians on film. A veteran of the silent era, Cody appeared in hundreds of westerns during the 1930s, 1940s, and 1950s. In most of these films, Indians appeared as savage villains, despite Cody's efforts to encourage his directors to present a more balanced view of Indian-and-white conflicts. Happily, his acting career lasted long enough for him to benefit from a turnabout in Hollywood's depiction of Indians in the 1960s and 1970s. Largely because of the civil rights movement, which had forced whites to examine their historic discrimination of African Americans and other minorities, movies that depicted Indians in a sympathetic light started to find an audience. As a result, in his final films, Cody at last had the opportunity to play several memorable and realistic Indian characters.

During the 1960s, minority performers in all media began to enjoy a newfound popularity. As the battle for civil rights broke down racial barriers, many of these artists were given their first

Iron Eyes Cody and non-Indian film star Jeff Chandler in Broken Arrow *(1950). During his long career, Cody helped to break down many Hollywood conventions, including the common practice of hiring white actors to play sympathetic Indian characters.* (Courtesy of the Museum of Modern Art Film Stills Archive)

At once flamboyant and reflective, singer-songwriter Buffy Sainte-Marie has spent her career challenging her audiences to reexamine their preconceptions about the world and their place in it. (Courtesy of EMI Records Group)

chance to play to a mainstream white audience, who responded to their gifts with enthusiasm. Popular music was particularly energized by this emergence of new talent. Rock was shaped largely by African-American singers and musicians, while folk, traditionally the music of protest, embraced talented artists from nearly every American minority group.

Among the most popular folk singer-songwriters was the multitalented Buffy Sainte-Marie, who, fresh out of college, became a star of the modern folk music boom of the early 1960s. By the age of 25, Sainte-Marie had written nearly two hundred songs on a variety of subjects. To the press and much of the public, however, she was identified with only the handful of her songs that protested injustices committed against Indian people. Herself a Cree Indian active in the Indian rights movement, Sainte-Marie was disconcerted by her frequent billing as an Indian singer. She recognized with dismay that her Indianness made her seem fashionable to a sizable portion of her white audience. Some of her most ardent fans came to concerts more to appear stylish than to listen to her music. As Sainte-Marie said to a *Ms.* magazine reporter in 1975, "Those angry songs just made people clap; nobody ever did anything about Indians."

Sainte-Marie's skepticism is largely shared by her friend John Trudell, who, as the national chairman of the American Indian Movement, was on the front lines of the battle for Indian rights during the 1970s. As the American public became more conservative in the following decade, Trudell abandoned his confidence in political activism as a catalyst for rapid social change. He has since traded in his life as an activist for that of an artist. His powerful and intelligent spoken-word recordings, many of which reflect the difficulties Indians face today as an American minority, are quickly developing a growing following.

To Trudell's discomfort, the popular interest in his work has been inspired in part by the success of the 1989 film *Dances With Wolves*, a historical drama that presents a fairly idyllic view of traditional Sioux Indian society. In a 1992 interview with *Request* magazine, Trudell condemned the film as "dangerous to [Indians] in the long run. It's a romantic movie about our past, which makes

John Trudell as Indian activist Jimmy Looks Twice in the 1992 film
Thunderheart. (Courtesy of the Museum of Modern Art Film Stills
Archive)

the Indian and his and her problems invisible in the present."

Graham Greene, the Oneida Indian actor who won unanimous acclaim for his performance as Kicking Bird in the film, is much more charitable toward *Dances*. He is proud of his contribution to a movie that has inspired many people, including himself, to learn more about native cultures. Yet, sharing Trudell's concern that contemporary Indians are rarely seen on film, Greene also has made a point of seeking out roles in which he plays Indian men living in the present. In the future, he hopes as well to play more non-Indian characters—a goal dependent on filmmakers' ability to learn to look beyond the fine Indian actor to see something even more obvious, the fine actor.

All of the profiles in this book tell a dual story. On one hand, each provides the details of a performer's life and work, with particular attention to the ways in which their experiences as a North American Indian have affected their art. On the other hand, the profiles present a picture of their audiences, the Indians who

FBI agents harassing an Indian policeman portrayed by Graham Greene in a scene from Thunderheart. *The film reversed the roles traditionally played by Indians and non-Indians in movie westerns by depicting radical Indian leaders as heroes and non-Indian lawmen as villains.* (Courtesy of the Museum of Modern Art Film Stills Archive)

have been inspired by the performers' example and the non-Indians who, rightly or wrongly, often have drawn conclusions about all Indian peoples from their impressions of a single performer on stage, on film, or on record. As the cultural guardians of their people, traditional Indian performers certainly had an awesome responsibility. But as the most public representatives of the Indian minority to the non-Indian majority, the burden of these modern Indian performers in many ways has been even greater.

EMILY PAULINE JOHNSON

◆ ◆ ◆

Mohawk Actress
(1861–1913)

Pauline Johnson watched from the wings as the audience filed into the auditorium of Toronto's Academy of Music. The evening's program had been advertised as a recital of poetry celebrating Canada, but Johnson knew that most of the crowd had been lured by the names of the famous poets on the roster, many of whom had had their works published by newspapers and magazines with circulations in the millions. Johnson's achievements were far more modest. Only a handful of her poems had appeared in small journals, and she had never read her work in public. Still, Frank Yeigh, the old school friend who had organized the readings, had assured her that she could hold her own among the seasoned professionals he had scheduled.

The first three speakers received a warm reception, but only polite applause after their overlong, uninspired readings. Sensing the restlessness of the crowd, Johnson felt a wave of nervousness as her name was announced as the next recitalist. However, as she made her way to the podium, the crowd did not see the terrified amateur she imagined herself to appear, but, instead, an elegant

*A publicity still of Johnson dressed in one of the evening gowns she wore during
the second portion of her readings.* (Brant County Museum and Archives)

young woman with dark brown hair, gray eyes, olive skin, and
delicate features. Her simple gray evening gown and impeccable
posture gave her an aristocratic demeanor. To the audience, Johnson looked like an English gentlewoman.

Only when she began to speak did she betray her inexperience.
The other readers had used vocal tricks and exaggerated gestures

to enhance their performances, but Johnson interpreted her material purely through her own emotions. Although her delivery was at times halting and hesitant, the obvious sincerity of her reading more than made up for its lack of sophistication.

Even more striking than her stage presence were the words she spoke. Reciting from her poem "A Cry from an Indian Wife," she acted out the role of its narrator, an Indian woman who is sending her husband into battle during the North West Rebellion of 1885. In this conflict, 300 Indians in Saskatchewan, Canada, fought 8,000 Canadian troops in an unsuccessful attempt to retain control of their ancestral homeland.

The poem traces the wife's conflicting emotions about the rebellion. At first, she rallies her husband to fight, but hesitates as she finds herself sympathizing with the enemy. She admits that the soldiers "all are young and beautiful and good" and that, although they have helped the government seize Indian land, "their new rule and council is well meant." Yet, as she comes to see the conflict from the soldiers' perspective, she also acknowledges the enemy's refusal even to try to understand the Indians' point of view:

> They never think how they would feel to-day,
> If some great nation came from far away,
> Wresting their country from their hapless braves,
> Giving what they gave us—but wars and graves.

Her anger grows until she finally urges her husband to:

> Go forth, nor bend to greed of white men's hands,
> By right, by birth we Indians own these lands.

As Johnson finished these lines, the room was dead quiet. She paused a moment, unsure of what to do next, then nodded to the audience to indicate her reading was over. As she moved to exit the stage, the audience broke out in wild applause and cries of "encore." Yeigh later claimed that Johnson's debut had transformed his literary evening from a disaster to the most important cultural event in Canada that season. No less effervescent in his praise, a reviewer for the *Toronto Globe* wrote that Johnson "was like the voice of the nations who have wasted away before our civilization speaking through this cultured, gifted, soft-voiced descendant."

◆ ◆ ◆

Emily Pauline Johnson was born on March 10, 1861, on the Six Nations Reserve near Brantford, Ontario. The youngest in a family of four children, she was the daughter of George Henry Martin Johnson, a Mohawk leader, and Emily Susanna Howells, a white woman who had been born in Bristol, England.

On her father's side, Pauline was descended from one of the original founders of the Iroquois Confederacy, a powerful league of five Indian tribes that was formed in the late 16th century (later joined by another tribe to become the Six Nations). Her ancestors had lived in what is now upstate New York until just after the American Revolution (1775–83). Because the Mohawks had sided with the English during the conflict, many fled to British-held Canada after the American colonists' victory. These Indians, led by Mohawk chief Joseph Brant, were given a tract named the Six Nations Reserve in the Grand River Valley as a reward for their loyalty to the English Crown.

The Grand River Mohawks were pro-British largely because of the influence of Sir William Johnson, who long served as the English government's superintendent of Indian affairs in North America. Before his death in 1774, Johnson invited Pauline's great-grandfather to take his surname as his own, an honor that reflected the distinguished position her family held among both Indians and whites in the region.

Reared to be an Iroquois leader, George Johnson was taught to love and revere the traditions of the Mohawks. However, his father and Pauline's grandfather—noted orator John "Smoke" Johnson—also insisted that George attend an English-run school. Because of his subsequent mastery of the English language, George later was hired as an interpreter by the Christian missionaries who lived among the Mohawks. Soon after taking this post, he was named to the Grand Council, the governing body of the confederacy. These two positions gave George Johnson considerable power in the affairs of the reserve.

While visiting the home of a local reverend, he met Emily Howells. The two fell in love, and, over the objections of both of their families, they married in 1853. George then moved his bride to a two-hundred acre estate on the Grand River that he called Chiefswood. The house he had built there was impressive enough to earn him a new Mohawk name—Onwanonsyshon, or "He Who Has the Great Mansion."

In an essay titled "My Mother," Pauline Johnson recounted the many shared interests that brought her parents together: "They loved nature—the trees, best of all, and the river, and the birds. They loved the Anglican Church; they loved the British flag; they loved Queen Victoria. . . . They loved music, pictures, and dainty china, with which George filled his beautiful home. . . . but, most of all, these two loved the Indian people." According to Canadian law, Pauline's mother became an Indian when she married George Johnson; however, Emily Johnson's Indianness was more than a legal designation. According to Pauline, her mother was also a Mohawk "by the sympathies and yearnings and affections of her own heart."

Nevertheless, Emily Johnson insisted on passing on to her children many of the values she learned during her own upbringing. Like many women reared in Victorian England, she was almost obsessive in her demands for cleanliness and order. She insisted that her children develop self-discipline and carry themselves with the dignity befitting young ladies and gentlemen of England's upper class.

With few playmates other than her brothers and sister, Pauline spent much of her childhood alone in her parents' library. As a young girl, she taught herself to read. By the age of 12, she had poured through many of the classics of English and American literature, including the works of William Shakespeare, Lord Byron, and Henry Wadsworth Longfellow. All the while, Pauline learned about the Mohawks' history and legends from her father and paternal grandfather.

After three years at an Indian school on the reserve, 14-year-old

Pauline was sent to Brantford Collegiate, a nearby boarding school. There she began acting in plays and pageants. When she returned home two years later, she announced that she had found her calling and intended to become a professional actress. Her parents strongly discouraged her new ambition. Acting was then considered far too tawdry an occupation for someone of her social class and distinguished lineage.

Instead, Pauline Johnson busied herself with writing poetry, which both she and her parents saw more as a diversion rather than a career. In her own estimation, Johnson was merely biding her time while waiting for a proposal of marriage from an appropriate suitor. Although she was courted by many men, none lived up to her expectations. Johnson tended to idealize her parents' marriage and wanted no less than the complete melding of hearts and minds that their union represented to her. She also considered only white men as possible husbands, which in view of her Indian heritage limited the number of her marriage candidates. Unions between whites and Indians were then considered unconventional, if not shocking, to most upper-class white families.

After the death of Johnson's father in 1884, her family's income dwindled. To help earn her keep, she began publishing a few of her poems in small newspapers and journals and took to signing her works with "Tekahionwake," the Mohawk name of her grandfather, Smoke Johnson. Over the next seven years, Johnson's writing garnered her enough attention to make her a local celebrity, but the income it yielded was disappointing. Between 1884 and 1891, she received less than a total of $100 from the sale of her work. During these years, Johnson grew tired both of relying on her older sister for financial support and of trying to find new amusements to fill her idle time.

In January 1892, Frank Yeigh, a former classmate, offered Johnson a chance to break out of her routine. He asked her to read some of her poems at a recital he was organizing for the Young Men's Liberal Club of Ontario. The other readers he scheduled were well-known in Canada's literary cliques. Yeigh hoped that a relative unknown would add some novelty to the program.

At first, Johnson balked at his invitation, but Yeigh's faith in her talents helped her overcome her initial shyness. The idea of performing at a recital in the company of noted writers also held great appeal to Johnson. As a recitalist, she could experience the joy of acting before an audience without endangering her social position.

Just as Yeigh had expected, Johnson's debut was a great success. After the crowd cheered her recitation of "A Cry from an Indian Wife," Johnson read "As Red Men Die," a poem that tells the story of an Iroquois man who is about to be tortured by warriors from the Huron tribe, the Iroquois's greatest traditional enemies. In the poem, the stoic Iroquois captive takes comfort in knowing that his tribespeople will avenge his death:

> His vile detested captors, that now flaunt
> Their war clubs in his face with sneer and taunt,
> Not thinking, soon that reeking, red, and raw,
> Their scalps will deck the belts of Iroquois.

Here, as in much of her writing on Indian themes, Johnson presented Indian warfare in the goriest terms possible in imitation of the many popular non-Indian authors who titillated readers with their descriptions of Indian "savagery." Unlike most of these writers, however, the gruesome scenes depicted by Johnson often had a basis in historical fact. For instance, the tortures described in "As Red Men Die" actually had been performed centuries earlier by the Hurons, who were notorious for the brutality with which they treated prisoners of war.

Impressed by Johnson's successful performance, Yeigh convinced his protégée to become a professional recitalist and to take him on as her manager. On a tour through towns and cities in eastern Canada, she gradually honed her act. At each performance, she recited a variety of poems, many of which celebrated the beauty of nature and the wonders of the Canadian countryside. But at Yeigh's urging, Johnson always included several of her poems on Indian themes. Yeigh suspected that many people paid admission to see a cultured Indian woman, a status that in some areas made Johnson a genuine curiosity.

To capitalize on this aspect of her performance, Yeigh billed her as "The Mohawk Princess." By the fall of 1892, Johnson also had begun dressing the part. During the first half of each performance, she wore a buckskin dress, a bear-claw necklace, woven bracelets of wampum (shell beads), and a feather in her hair. Crafted by Johnson herself, the costume reflected white ticket buyers' conception of what an "Indian princess" would wear rather than of the traditional dress of any particular Indian group. After an intermission, Johnson reappeared dressed in an evening gown to read her works on non-Indian subjects.

Like most recitalists, Johnson traveled with a musician who entertained the audience with a few songs before her performance. For five years, a British pianist named Owen Smiley provided her opening act. A veteran of English music halls, Smiley was familiar with the workings of show business. As he and Johnson became friends, he taught her how to judge and play to her audiences and when to inject comic interludes in her monologues.

The two performers also worked together on a dramatization of Johnson's story "A Red Girl's Reasoning," which became the most popular portion of their program. In the short play, Smiley had the role of a Canadian official who marries a beautiful Indian woman played by Johnson. When the wife makes a casual reference to her white father and Indian mother's marriage by Indian rites, her husband is scandalized. In his view, because her parents were not married in a Christian church, she is illegitimate, a judgment she finds appalling. She angrily leaves her husband, explaining, "I tell you we are not married. Why should I recognize the rites of your nation when you do not acknowledge the rites of mine?" As in "A Cry from an Indian Wife," the young Indian bride is willing to respect white customs only as long as whites respect Indian ways.

"A Red Girl's Reasoning" also challenged a then popular convention of women's fiction. Melodramatic stories of love between an Indian woman and a white man were common in the late 19th century. Read primarily by middle-class non-Indian women who felt uncomfortable with marriage across racial lines, these romances generally ended in tragedy and most often with

Emily Pauline Johnson wearing her Indian performance costume. Johnson often asked to be photographed in profile in order to draw attention to her nose, her most Indian-like feature. (Brant County Museum and Archives)

the suicide of the Indian woman. Johnson consciously played against convention by leaving her heroine not only alive but defiant. The Indian woman's tale concludes with a bold declaration of freedom: "Neither church, nor law, nor even love can make a slave of a red girl."

As Johnson's success as a performer grew, so did the disapproval of her family. To them and to herself, she justified her show business career as a means of funding the publication of her poetry. Johnson promised to end her tours when she had earned enough money to travel to London to find a publisher. Influenced strongly by the work of British poets, she felt her work should be sold through an English publishing house if she were to receive the respect she longed for in established literary circles.

In April 1894, Johnson finally arrived in London with a satchel full of letters of introduction. With these notes from friends and acquaintances vouching for her charm and good breeding, she came to know the cream of London society and was invited to perform her act in drawing rooms throughout the city. Before returning to Canada in July, Johnson used her new international fame to land a contract with Bodley Head, England's premier publisher of poetry. A year later, Johnson's first volume of poems, *The White Wampum,* appeared to good reviews.

Back in Canada, Johnson realized that financially she could not afford to give up performing and embarked on a tour through the western provinces. Appearing mostly in rural areas and small towns, Johnson discovered that many people who came to these recitals had disturbing misconceptions about Indians' appearance and behavior. Their concepts of Indians had been culled largely from popular fiction that portrayed Indians as hostile and savage peoples. They had difficulty reconciling these ideas with the cultured and sophisticated persona presented by Johnson. To help counteract the stereotypes of her audiences, Johnson took to proclaiming her Indianness frequently and loudly. In much of her publicity material, she insisted on being photographed in profile in order to emphasize her nose, her one facial feature that most whites recognized as Indian-like.

On a tour through the United States in 1896, Johnson found that Americans in the West were even more prejudiced. In the late 19th century, both the popular press and the U.S. government promoted the hatred of western Indian groups by portraying Indians as wild and violent killers. To Johnson's disgust, many Americans came to her performances to gawk at her as they would a freak in a sideshow. Following a trip through Michigan, she declared that everyone she met in the state was "very uncultured, very ignorant, very illiterate," an assessment that encapsulated her opinion of most of the Americans she encountered.

When their American tour ended, Johnson and Smiley decided to dissolve their partnership. The event ushered in a difficult period for Johnson. Determined to travel less, she tried settling in Winnipeg. There she became engaged to a younger man, who broke off their relationship when his family objected to his marrying an entertainer. Several months before this rejection, Johnson's mother died. During this time, her career also began to flounder. A new manager convinced her to spend much of her savings on expensive promotions and probably also stole a considerable sum from her before she dismissed him.

Desperate for money, Johnson began touring again in 1901 with a new partner, J. Walter McRaye. Although less talented than Smiley, McRaye was a pleasant companion, and his enthusiastic admiration for Johnson gave her a badly needed dose of confidence. Together they traveled throughout Canada, playing in saloons, mining camps, and fishing villages as well as theaters. To please the relatively unsophisticated audiences in frontier areas, Johnson relied increasingly on acting out parodies of high society and joking with the crowd. Although she felt uncomfortable with clowning, she rationalized it by claiming that the more sober portions of her program taught at least some of the audience members to appreciate poetry.

In part to bolster her creditability as a serious poet, Johnson published her second book of poems, *Canadian Born,* in 1902. The volume was not well received. Her many years on the road had left her with little time to polish her writing. Most reviewers complained that the new poems were technically clumsy and lacked the honest emotion of her earlier works. Johnson was so dispirited by the book's reception that she abandoned poetry and began concentrating on writing stories about Indian life, which she discovered were far easier to sell to magazines than her poems had been.

Johnson and McRaye continued touring in Canada and went to England for brief engagements in 1906 and 1907. They also found a new audience for their act at chautauquas. These summertime lecture programs were popular in the eastern United States and featured speeches by luminaries such as Ralph Waldo Emerson, Nathaniel Hawthorne, and William Jennings Bryan. Often in ill health, Johnson found working at chautauquas wearing. Her growing impatience and irritation came out in a conversation with a reporter in Boston in 1907. During the interview, Johnson snapped, "Ah, I understand that look. You're going to say I'm not like other Indians, that I'm not representative. That's not strange. Cultivate an Indian, let him show his aptness, and you Americans say he is an exception. Let a bad quality crop out, and you stamp him as an Indian immediately." When McRaye told her in 1909 that he wanted to leave the act to get married, she was relieved, seeing his departure as an convenient excuse to retire from show business.

Johnson decided to settle in Vancouver, British Columbia, where she devoted herself to writing stories. She became a regular contributor to *Mother's Magazine*, a periodical featuring advice on child care and information about women's rights with a circulation of more than half a million. Most of Johnson's stories for the magazine dealt with the struggles and triumphs of Indian women. Johnson also wrote children's tales about Canadian trappers and mounties for *Boy's World* and her own versions of the legends of Pacific Coast Indians for the *Vancouver Province*.

Soon after her retirement from show business, Johnson was diagnosed with breast cancer. Even when she was at her most productive, making a living from her fiction was hard, but as the disease spread and writing became more difficult, Johnson could no longer earn enough money to pay for food or her meager lodgings. Her wealthy friends in Vancouver wanted to help but knew that Johnson would refuse their charity. Instead, they published her Indian myths in a book titled *Legends of Vancouver* (1911) and arranged for her to receive the proceeds from its sale. Following the success of this project, Johnson's friends collected her poetry from *The White Wampum* and *Canadian Born* as well as some previous unpublished verse into a single volume, *Flint and Feather* (1912). They went on to create collections of her *Mother's Magazine* stories (*The Moccasin Maker*, 1913) and her *Boy's World* pieces (*The*

Shagganappi, 1913), but Johnson did not live to see their publication. On March 7, 1913, she died in her home at the age of 51.

◆ ◆ ◆

In her final days, Johnson directed that "no tombstone or monument be raised in my memory, as I prefer to be remembered in the hearts of my people and my public." But within only a few years after her death, the public's memory of Johnson was quickly fading. The unprecedented carnage of World War I (1914–18) so shocked American and European soldiers and civilians that older literary styles no longer seemed adequate vehicles for communicating the tragedies and confusions of modern life. As writers experimented with new means of expression, poetry as deeply rooted in 19th-century traditions as Johnson's rapidly came to appear too dated to speak to most contemporary readers.

Her reputation fared better in the 1920s, when Canadian nationalists sparked a movement to promote awareness of the country's literary heritage. Johnson emerged as one of this movement's heroes. Her poems were featured prominently in many anthologies and textbooks that celebrated Canadian literature. For several generations, nearly every Canadian schoolchild was asked to commit at least one of Johnson's poems to memory.

In more recent years, Johnson's work has again fallen into obscurity. However, her colorful life and forceful personality continue to elicit excitement, especially among feminist scholars and writers. They laud her success in an extremely demanding profession and her daring in seeking financial self-sufficiency in an era when women were expected to live off the earnings of the men they married.

By emphasizing her life over her writing, Johnson's audience today differs little from those of the past. Although Johnson was reluctant to admit it, relatively few people paid admission to her shows because they were eager to receive the dose of culture she offered. Some came to stare at an Indian woman; some wanted to look at a sophisticated lady in a pretty dress; others just wanted an hour's diversion. Through her energy and passion as a performer and her ability to coax her audience to reconsider their notions about femininity and Indianness, Johnson gave them all more than their money's worth.

LUTHER
STANDING BEAR

◆ ◆ ◆

Teton Sioux Wild West
Performer and Film Actor
(c. 1868–1939)

The vast arena was filled long before the show was to begin. Only a few seats decorated with gold paint in the center remained empty. The audience waited quietly until it spied a group of gentlemen in black evening clothes and silk hats and gentlewomen in lovely dresses with long trains enter the arena and make their way to the gilded section. Amid the excited murmuring of the crowd, the seats with the very best view were taken by a large, bearded man and an elegant woman with a jeweled tiara and necklace. Backstage, word quickly spread that the king and queen of England had finally arrived.

In a moment, the announcer's voice came over the loudspeaker, offering everyone a grand welcome to Buffalo Bill's Wild West Show. After promising to thrill the audience with a dazzling spectacle, he introduced the stars of the show, who, one by one, came forward to join a parade around the arena.

The climax of the procession was the appearance of the Indian warriors. As the announcer called out "The Sioux Nation," about

20 young men mounted on jet black horses raced into the arena. The Sioux were dressed in colorful, beaded buckskin outfits and feathered headdresses that were so long that they nearly scraped the ground. As the Sioux were joined by the "The Cheyenne Nation" and "The Arapaho Nation," the arena was filled with fabulously costumed Indians, each trying to upstage the others with his skill as a horseman.

Into this crowd, at the bequest of the announcer, rode the "Chief Interpreter of the Sioux," known offstage as Luther Standing Bear. Outside of the world of the Wild West show, Standing Bear was not in fact the Sioux's official interpreter. By 1902, when he joined an English tour of Buffalo Bill's production, no such title existed, but his introduction was by no means the program's only deception. A tiny part fact and a huge part fancy, the show depicted a fantasy version of the Sioux Nation. In reality, by that time, the traditional world of the Sioux in which Standing Bear had been born and reared had been all but destroyed.

◆ ◆ ◆

According to the Teton Sioux calendar, Luther Standing Bear was born in "the year of the breaking up of camp" and in "the month when the bark of the trees cracked." By his own calculations, his birth month was December of the year 1868, the end of a momentous year in the history of his people. Led by the great leader Red Cloud, Teton warriors began waging a guerrilla war against the U.S. Army in the mid-1860s. These soldiers had come to the Indians' homeland in the Great Plains in order to protect wagon trains of American prospectors and settlers heading westward. Always resentful of intruders, the Tetons had battled so fiercely and so relentlessly that the U.S. government was forced to sue for peace. The result was the Treaty of Fort Laramie of 1868, in which the U.S. forces agreed to abandon their forts in Teton territory.

The Treaty of Fort Laramie represented a great victory for the Tetons. Although the war for the Plains would soon resume, for the time being, they had stalled the non-Indian infiltration of their lands. For Luther Standing Bear and other Sioux of his generation, the brief peace meant that they could grow up relatively free from the interference of whites.

In *My Indian Boyhood,* Standing Bear's 1931 account of his youth, he described his traditional Teton Sioux childhood. Its highlight was his first and only buffalo hunt, an event that signaled the beginning of his adulthood. Like most Indian tribes of the Great Plains, the Tetons revered successful hunters because buffalo kills helped maintain their way of life. From the buffalo, the tribe derived most of its food, the materials for its clothing and shelters, and many other necessities.

In the traditional Sioux world, training as a warrior was equally as crucial to a boy's development. The Teton Sioux greatly respected skilled warriors, whom they entrusted with the vital responsibility of guarding their territory. Standing Bear's father had become powerful among the Brulé, a subtribe of the Tetons, in part because of his reputation as a fighter. The boy's Indian name, Ota Kte (Plenty Kill), was a tribute to his father's success in battling the Tetons' Indian enemies.

By the time Ota Kte came of age, however, the opportunities for young Teton men to prove themselves in battle were nonexistent. According to the terms of past treaties, the Sioux were confined to several reservations overseen by U.S. government employees known as agents. Agents outlawed raids and skirmishes among Plains Indian groups, thus blocking an important means for young Sioux men to gain the respect of their peers. These laws were just one part of a larger campaign engineered by agents to intimidate Indians and compel them to give up their tribal traditions.

In 1879, another group of non-Indians arrived in Sioux territory with hopes of reforming its residents. These whites were recruiters for the Carlisle Industrial Indian Boarding School, a new institution in Pennsylvania. The model for other boarding schools for Indians, Carlisle sought to instruct Indian children about the culture and manners of white America. With the encouragement of his father, who recognized that the Sioux's interaction with non-Indians was sure to increase, Ota Kte decided to attend the school.

At each train stop on the long journey to Carlisle, Ota Kte and his fellow recruits were greeted with the taunts of a crowd of non-Indians. More than 50 years later, in his 1934 memoir *Land of the Spotted Eagle,* Standing Bear recounted the terror he felt in one town as he walked from the train station to a restaurant: "I often recall that scene—80-odd blanketed boys and girls marching down the street surrounded by jeering, unsympathetic people whose only emotions were those of hate and fear; the conquerors looking upon the conquered."

Fresh in the minds of the "conquerors" was the Battle of Little Bighorn of 1876, the last substantial Indian victory of the Plains Wars. During this conflict, Teton Sioux warriors defeated U.S. soldiers led by General George Armstrong Custer. To solicit support for the U.S. Army's continuing campaign against the Plains Indians, newspaper accounts of the battle depicted the Indian warriors as bloodthirsty killers. These descriptions were accepted as true by many non-Indian Americans, particularly those who had profited from the seizure of Indian lands and were eager to have their consciences soothed.

Arriving at Carlisle provided little relief for Ota Kte. The teachers forbade him and the other Sioux children from speaking their own language. Because none of them knew English, they found themselves thousands of miles away from home and unable to communicate with anyone around them. In addition to coping with loneliness and fear, the students were faced with poor quality food, uncomfortable non-Indian clothing, and unhealthy accommodations. Worst of all, many students were exposed to European diseases to which they had little natural immunity. Standing Bear later wrote that "[within] three years nearly one half of the children from the Plains were dead and through with all earthly schools."

Perhaps influenced by a desire to please his father, Ota Kte became a model student at Carlisle. During his years there, he learned to speak English fluently, began using the name "Luther" as his teachers instructed him to do, and returned to the reservation several times to recruit new students.

After graduating, Luther Standing Bear returned to the

Rosebud Indian Reservation in present-day South Dakota. He quickly discovered that, in his absence, conditions at Rosebud had worsened. He later wrote that the reservation then seemed like "the Garden of Eden after the fall of man." Agents had gained even greater power over the Sioux, who increasingly were forced to rely on small food rations supplied by the U.S. government. The Indians' own economy, particularly their ability to obtain food, had declined with the buffalo population, which had been decimated by white hunters.

On the reservation, most Carlisle graduates looking to make a living discovered that their education was practically worthless. However, because of his excellent scholastic record, Standing Bear was able to land a job as an assistant teacher at a local school. While working there, Standing Bear married, started a family, and became an advocate of a U.S. government policy known as allotment. The allotment policy encouraged the breaking up of Indian reservations, which were owned in common by all residents, into small plots (called allotments) that could become the private property of individual Indians. Standing Bear felt that if Indians emulated whites by becoming private landowners, the Sioux would have a better chance of preventing non-Indians from taking over their territory.

Despite his support for allotment, Standing Bear had little sympathy for most other U.S. government policies and practices involving the Sioux. Particularly horrifying to him was the 1890 massacre of more than 150 unarmed Sioux women, men, and children by U.S. troops near Wounded Knee Creek, an event that signaled the Indians' final defeat in the Plains Wars. Recording his reaction to news of the catastrophe, Standing Bear wrote, "It made my blood boil. . . . There I was, doing my best to teach my people to follow the white men's road—even trying to get them to believe in their religion—and this was my reward for it all!"

Because he knew and trusted the agent at the nearby Pine Ridge Indian Reservation, Standing Bear soon moved his family there. As he looked for work on Pine Ridge and in surrounding towns, Standing Bear discovered that, however lacking his Carlisle education had been, it had given him a valuable sense of how to

A 1907 publicity photograph of William "Buffalo Bill" Cody and the Indian performers in his Wild West show. (Wyoming State Museum)

function in both Indian and non-Indian society. With this training, he was able to take on a wide variety of jobs. Over the next decade, Standing Bear found work as a store manager, an agency clerk, a minister's assistant, and a rancher.

In 1902, while Standing Bear was managing a store in Allen, South Dakota, a friend suggested that he pursue still another line of work by applying for a job as an interpreter for Buffalo Bill's Wild West Show. "Buffalo Bill" was the stage name of William Cody, who had been an army scout and guide before entering show business. When Cody founded his traveling show in 1883, it featured little more than displays of trick riding and sharpshooting. As its popularity and Cody's ambitiousness grew, he began to stage "spectacles"—reenactments of historical events, particularly battles between Indians and army soldiers, that were often depicted in popular fiction about the West. In order to made these dramas seem more authentic, he often hired Indians and former U.S. soldiers as players.

Standing Bear claimed he ultimately decided to take a job with Cody on a dare. However, more likely, the reasons behind his decision were similar to those of any other Sioux performers who signed up for the show. The salary was attractive, especially because earning a living wage was difficult for reservation residents. The chance to travel and work in show business also offered Cody's employees some excitement. But perhaps the most important incentive was the freedom the job represented. On reservations, Indians grew weary of the orders of agents, most of whom abused their power. Particularly for Indians whom agents had branded as troublemakers, performing in the Wild West show provided a welcome respite from petty rules and regulations.

Nearly unique among Indian Wild West performers, Standing Bear left behind a record of his experiences with the show in his 1928 memoirs, *My People, the Sioux.* According to his account, he was hired by Cody to act as an interpreter, but the extent of his duties and responsibilities were not clear. He eventually decided that, as the most fluent English speaker among the 75 Sioux on the tour, he was in charge of making sure the Indians showed up for performances and were not distracted or led astray in any way by the non-Indians they encountered.

In the show itself, Standing Bear played the "Chief Interpreter of the Sioux Nation" during a procession of the Indian performers. As they paraded before the audience, the Sioux actors depicted warriors from four different tribes. Because popular novels had familiarized his audiences with the names of such Plains Indian groups as the Cheyennes and the Arapahos, Cody knew his customers were eager to see Indians from those tribes as well as the Sioux. Rather than expending the effort to recruit Cheyennes and Arapahos, the showman merely billed his favored Sioux performers as members of these groups.

Occasionally, Standing Bear was asked to join the non-Indian performers in playing the part of a cowboy. His admission that he "enjoyed [the role] very much" was telling. As he knew from bitter experience, on the reservation a person's status as an Indian or non-Indian determined almost everything about their life and their future. In show business, however, racial distinctions became blurred. By allowing Indians to play non-Indians and vice versa, the world of the Wild West show offered Standing Bear a position of equality with whites that was difficult to find elsewhere.

Not surprisingly, much of Standing Bear's account of the tour focused on the privileges accorded to him as a show personality. He was especially appreciative of the regard Cody extended to his Indian performers. In one anecdote, Standing Bear recalled an evening meal during which the Indian performers were fed leftover pancakes, while the non-Indians in the show were served a freshly prepared dinner. After he complained about the Indians' treatment, Cody immediately marched to the cook and said: "I want you to understand, sir, that I will not stand for such treatment. My Indians are the principal feature of this show, and they are the one people I will not allow to be misused or neglected. Hereafter see to it that they get just exactly what they want at meal-time." This guarantee undoubtedly meant a great deal to people who were accustomed to inadequate and unhealthy government rations.

Standing Bear's narrative also concentrated on the deference bestowed on the Indian performers by the English. For instance, with obvious delight, he recounted his discovery that a well-dressed English gentlemen found poking through the Sioux's possessions at one hotel was hired to make the Indians' beds. In retelling this and similar stories, Standing Bear expected his readers to respond with surprise that Englishmen and Englishwomen, whom many Americans then believed to be their own social and cultural superiors, would work as servants to Indians.

After 11 months in England, Standing Bear returned to Pine Ridge. The next spring he accepted an invitation to join the Wild West show for another European tour, but he was injured in a major train wreck en route. Unable to travel, he lost his spot in the show.

In the following years, Standing Bear spent most of his time working in various western towns and cities. Even though he was rarely on the reservation, he remained active in the politics of Pine Ridge, especially in debates over allotment. On a personal level, Standing Bear supported allotment because he wanted to secure as much land for himself as possible. In fact, he was so eager to obtain additional allotments that he traveled to Washington, D.C., in 1912 in order to plead his case before the commissioner of the Bureau of Indian Affairs, the head of the government agency charged with all official dealings with Indian people.

Many Sioux, lacking the funds or initiative needed for such a trip, found that their applications for allotments were ignored. Their frustration turned to rage when government officials began making arrangements to sell Pine Ridge's "surplus land," the U.S. government's term for any land left over after all qualified reservation residents had received allotments. Sioux leaders quickly organized a commission to travel to Washington to prevent the government's premature sale of their land. Standing Bear was eager to join the group but was blocked by local agents, who resented that he had gone over their heads when bargaining for his own share of tribal territory. The experience was so disheartening that Standing Bear decided to leave Pine Ridge and abandon politics.

Uncertain about what to do next, Standing Bear wrote to Thomas Ince, a silent film producer, in 1912. Ince worked for Bison 101, a movie studio based near Santa Monica, California, that specialized in filming stories about the West. The film industry was then in its infancy, but already westerns had emerged as America's most popular movie genre.

Early western films drew heavily on specific scenes and the overall sense of spectacle created by Buffalo Bill's Wild West Show and its imitators. Whereas moviegoers enjoyed seeing familiar western stories portrayed through the new medium of film, filmmakers were attracted to the genre in part because of the large pool of available and experienced talent found in the casts of Wild West extravaganzas. Impressed by Standing Bear's credentials as one of Buffalo Bill's favorite performers, Ince agreed to hire him as an actor. Standing Bear then moved to California, where he spent many years working for Ince and other noted western moviemakers.

When he was unable to line up movie work, Standing Bear traveled from town to town on the lecture circuit. His speeches attracted non-Indians who wished to hear a more factual account

Surrounded by Sioux Indian movie extras, Luther Standing Bear shakes hands with silent film director Thomas Ince in this 1914 photograph. (Bison Archives)

of Indian life and ways than the Wild West shows or filmed westerns were offering. Standing Bear's success as a lecturer inspired him to write books about his experiences and the traditions of his people. In addition to two books for children—*My Indian Boyhood* and *Stories of the Sioux* (1934)—he published two memoirs. The first, *My People, the Sioux,* was a relatively light-hearted account of Standing Bear's life prior to his move to California; the second, *Land of the Spotted Eagle,* focused on the changes that had occurred in Sioux society as a result of their contact with whites.

Standing Bear's most politically charged book, *Spotted Eagle,* was published on the eve of a major change in the U.S. government's policy concerning Indians. In 1934, Congress passed the Indian Reorganization Act, which was intended to correct many of the abuses committed against Indian populations in the past. Its most important provisions established guidelines

for the creation of tribal governments, thereby limiting the authority of U.S. employees on reservations, and brought an end to
allotment. Contrary to Standing Bear's expectations, the allotment
policy had allowed non-Indians to take control of millions of acres
of Indian land.

Many Indians were heartened by these reforms, but in *Spotted
Eagle,* Standing Bear expressed only skepticism for the
government's latest ideas for bettering the lives of Indians. Having seen firsthand the disappointing results of the Indian education movement and the allotment policy, Standing Bear
questioned any plan created by non-Indian officials. In *Spotted
Eagle,* he blamed whites' "tyranny, stupidity, and lack of vision"
for the poverty of most Indian people.

In the book's final chapters, Standing Bear made his own pro-
posals for improving reservation life. Among his suggestions
were requiring that all American students study Indian history
and supporting the education of Indian historians, doctors, and
other professionals. Ignored at the time, these innovations were
finally explored by the U.S. government beginning in the late
1960s.

Another of Standing Bear's targets in *Spotted Eagle* was the
popular entertainment industry and the distorted image of Indians that it presented to the American public. He complained that
"lurid fiction, cheap magazines, motion pictures, and newspapers
help impart the wrong idea that a scalp and a war dance are
counterparts of native American life, while the truth is but not
recorded." In his critique, however, Standing Bear neglected to
mention his own participation in Wild West shows and in movie
westerns. After writing these words, he continued to take occasional acting jobs in the movie industry until he died in 1939 while
filming the western epic *Union Pacific.*

◆ ◆ ◆

During Luther Standing Bear's lifetime, working in the entertainment industry was one of the few ways Sioux men could hope
to earn a steady income. In his early memoirs, Standing Bear
expressed pride in his performing career; but, as his hesitancy

even to mention this part of his life in his later works attests, his role as an entertainer eventually became an embarrassment. Standing Bear's literary success perhaps afforded him the luxury of feeling disdain toward show business. After his writing provided him with some attention and fame without compromising his dignity or integrity, performing lost its luster. At the end of his life, acting was little more than a decently paying, although somewhat humiliating, job.

The nature of the show business work available to him had changed as well. Despite its historical inaccuracies, the Wild West show at least had provided Indian performers with a forum in which they could earn the respect of a non-Indian audience. Based on what audiences had read or heard about Indians, many came to the shows expecting to gawk at primitive savages. Instead, they saw proud people dressed in beautifully decorated clothing and performing impressive feats of horsemanship.

The effect of this face-to-face contact was particularly evident in the reception given Sitting Bull—the great Sioux leader who became William Cody's biggest Indian star in 1885. Sitting Bull refused to participate in Cody's crude battle reenactments, so his part in the show was merely to ride on horseback through the arena. Some crowd members jeered the chief, who had often been depicted as a monster in press accounts of the Plains Wars. But, when confronted with his dignified comportment and personal charisma, just as many onlookers responded to his appearance with cheers and applause.

Although a few early western films attempted to tell stories of Indian people from their own perspective, most provided little opportunity for Indian performers to play a character or even to reveal their humanity. In fact, in the majority of westerns, Indians were treated more as props to add color to battle scenes than as actors with a role to play. The parts were no more cartoonish than those for Indians in Wild West shows, but, without the benefit of the physical presence of the performer, audiences felt far more distanced from Indian players on film. As Standing Bear rightly sensed, the distorted film image of Indians had become one of the greatest obstacles in their fight for rights. Movies had made many people so comfortable with seeing Native Americans only as celluloid villains that they could easily ignore flesh-and-blood Indians and their cries for justice.

WILL ROGERS

◆ ◆ ◆

Cherokee Humorist
(1879–1935)

In 1932, during a rare private moment, Will Rogers told a friend, politician James M. Cox, about one of his only career disappointments. Rogers was then a popular movie star, but despite his influence in Hollywood he could not sell his studio on the idea for a film he longed to make. The movie would tell the story of a country philosopher whose commonsense advice endeared him to his neighbors. In time, his fame spread until he was known and loved by every family in America. Then, suddenly, the country was plunged into economic and social chaos. As the only person the public trusted to see them through such turbulent times, the bumpkin found himself elected to the presidency.

Hollywood dismissed the idea as far-fetched, even subversive. Rogers, however, thought the movie could reveal both the good and the bad of the American political process. As Cox remembered, Rogers said, "It would not have lowered our institutions or government, in the public view, but it might have accomplished a good deal in showing that we should be pretty careful when the moods of our people take them to absurd lengths."

Rogers never made his movie, but in many ways he lived it. In films, on stage, and in newspaper columns, he pronounced simple and profound witticisms that helped Americans survive the brutality of the Great Depression. Unlike his character, however, Rogers rejected all suggestions that he run for office. He was embarrassed by the proposition, feeling a showman had no place trying to rule the country. But, in truth, he wielded nearly as much power as an entertainer as he could have as president. For many years, Rogers's fans looked to him to learn, by his example and by his instruction, how to be better Americans.

◆ ◆ ◆

Rogers once said, "My ancestors didn't come over on the *Mayflower*, but they met the boat." Actually his Cherokee forbears did not have any extended contact with whites until the mid-18th century, more than a hundred years after the Pilgrims landed. These whites were traders from England, Scotland, Germany, and Ireland. Among them were Rogers's two great-grandfathers, Irishman Robert Rogers and Welshman John Gunter, both of whom married Cherokee women.

Initially, the Cherokees welcomed the foreign traders into their homeland, which included most of present-day North and South Carolina, Georgia, Alabama, Tennessee, Virginia, and Kentucky. Although traditionally farmers and hunters, the Indians were eager to trade for European goods. They were also intrigued by the newcomers' customs and manners. Because of the Cherokees' willingness to adopt these new ways, whites began to regard them as the most "civilized" Indian group. After the formation of the United States, whites' attitude toward the Cherokees changed. Instead of admiring the Indians' industry and intelligence, officials started talking of the tribe as an obstacle to "progress." Led by President Andrew Jackson, federal and state officials announced their desire to take over the Cherokees' rich, lush land and open it to non-Indian settlers.

By the 1830s, their threats had grown far more ominous. Fearing an armed invasion if they refused, Cherokee leaders reluctantly agreed to the removal, or relocation, of the tribe to a region in the West designated as Indian Territory. The government scheduled the Cherokees' removal for 1838. The United States agreed to organize the tribe's exodus west, promising to provide adequate food and transportation for thousands of men, women, and children. However, some Cherokees were so leery of the government that they decided to make the trip on their own. Among these travelers, who later became known as the Old Settlers, was Will Rogers's paternal grandfather, Robert Rogers.

History bore out the wisdom of the Old Settlers' decision. By making their own arrangements for their relocation, they were able to take most of their possessions with them. The Cherokees they left behind were not so lucky. Forced in 1838 to leave their homes forever with nothing but the clothes on their backs, they had to suffer the horror of the Trail of Tears, as their journey to Indian Territory was called. The government's arrangements were so careless and provisions so meager that more than a quarter of the Cherokee population died along the way.

As one of the Old Settlers, Robert Rogers was able to lay claim to a tract of the choicest territory in the Cherokee Nation in the West (now northeastern Oklahoma). Although the dry land was ill-suited for farming, its thick covering of wild bluegrass made the area ideal for ranching. Robert Rogers became a rancher, and years later his son, Clement Vann Rogers, followed in his footsteps. Clem, his wife Mary, and their children settled on a huge V-shaped expanse spreading over hundreds of acres between the Caney and Verdigris rivers. There, Clem and his ranch hands raised thousands of head of cattle each year.

William Penn Adair Rogers, the couple's eighth and last child, was born on November 4, 1879. He was named after the assistant principal chief of the Cherokee Nation, under whom Clem had served on the side of the South during the Civil War.

Throughout his career, Will Rogers stressed his rural roots, often attributing his wisdom to a humble upbringing. For instance, in 1924, he wrote, "I am just an old country boy. I have been eating pretty regular, and the reason I have is I have stayed an old country boy." But contrary to his homespun persona, Rogers grew up in a wealthy family. In 1880, the first year Will was included on the official roll of the Cherokee tribe, Clem Rogers was the third richest man in Indian Territory. He was also powerful in local politics. Beginning in 1879, he served five terms in the Cherokee Senate.

Will Rogers remembered his early youth as idyllic. He spent his days playing with the Indian and African-American boys who lived nearby and watching the cowboys on his father's ranch. To the disappointment of his parents, he had far less enthusiasm for school. Like most Cherokees, the Rogerses greatly valued education. The tribe then owned and operated some of the best schools in the present-day United States.

At 18, Rogers decided he had enough education and ran away from the boarding school he had been attending. After two years of traveling and working as a ranch hand, he returned home to find that Indian Territory had changed. The U.S. government had once again seized control over Cherokee lands. Five years earlier, in 1893, the government had announced a plan to allot a small plot to each Cherokee man; all tribal land left over would be open to settlement by whites. Just before Will's return, he and Clem were finally granted their allotments. These tiny tracts amounted to only a fraction of the land needed to keep the family ranch operating. Always realistic, Clem Rogers sold most of his cattle and started a bank in the nearby town of Claremore.

Clem Rogers had seen the government's action coming years before. In 1883, he wrote in a letter to the Cherokees' principal chief, Dennis Bushyhead, "We are powerless to enforce our laws. . . . We are fast drifting into the hands of white men." But like many Cherokee leaders before him, Rogers also saw that change was inevitable. Instead of trying to stop it, he used his political influence to help his people deal with this time of transition.

Wanting to keep his son close to home, Clem gave Will the few cattle he still had. But life as a small rancher bored the young man. To amuse himself, Rogers started performing at roping contests. Although the era of the cowboy was coming to an end, Americans' fascination with the cowboy remained strong. At contests, skilled ropers could win cash prizes and the admiration of a large audience.

When he was 22, Rogers decided to strike out on his own for good. Hearing that younger ranchers could make a fortune in

The Greatest Catch in Vaudeville

Manipulating 90 ft of Rope.

As evident from this early publicity card, Rogers initially attracted a vaudeville audience solely on his talents as a trick roper. (From the archives of the Will Rogers Memorial, Claremore, Oklahoma)

Argentina, he and a friend set out for South America. When they arrived, they discovered that all the available ranching jobs had long since been taken by cowboys with more experience than they had. His friend left for home, but Rogers chose to travel on, determined to find a way to make a success of himself before going home to face his father.

He found work on a ship bound for South Africa and, upon his arrival, joined the cast of a Wild West show—a traveling demonstration of sharpshooting and trick riding and roping. He then traveled on to New Zealand, where he joined a circus and was billed as the "Cherokee Kid."

After Rogers returned to the United States in 1904, he briefly continued to work in Wild West shows, but their popularity was fading. Among the new forms of entertainment that were taking their place were variety shows on the vaudeville circuit. In time, Rogers started playing vaudeville shows in New York City. Wearing a cowboy outfit, he did a few rope tricks, then ended his set with the extremely difficult stunt of simultaneously roping a horse and its rider as they galloped across the stage. Originally, Rogers's was a "dumb act," meaning that he never spoke on stage. His silence ended after the horse's rider pointed out that Rogers performed the trick so quickly that the audience could not see what he had done. One night, he tried introducing the trick with, "I want to call your sho-nuff attention to this little stunt I am going to pull on you, as I am going to throw about two of these ropes at once, catching the horse with one and the rider with another." With its combination of western dialect and self-depreciating humor, the remark set the formula for Rogers's stage patter.

Rogers's success in New York led to jobs in vaudeville theaters all over the United States and Europe. During this time, he married his childhood sweetheart, Betty Blake. As they started a family, Rogers began looking for stable work in Broadway revues. In one show, he was spotted by a talent scout for Florenz Ziegfeld, then the best-known theater producer in the United States.

Rogers was hired to play first Ziegfeld's *Midnight Frolic* and later the *Ziegfeld Follies*. The drawing cards of both shows were their lavish production numbers. At first, Rogers's rope tricks were used to take up stage time while Ziegfeld's famous show girls were changing costume. But soon he developed a following of his own.

Rogers quickly saw that the fairly sophisticated audience for Ziegfeld's shows appreciated his repartee more than his rope twirling. He began talking more and more on stage, ad-libbing dozens of jokes to fill each of his 20-minute routines. Most of his material came from the day's headlines, especially during World

The most well-known publicity still of Rogers from his years as a star of the Ziegfeld Follies. (From the archives of the Will Rogers Memorial, Claremore, Oklahoma)

War I (1914–18) and its aftermath. His humor was particularly effective in deflating the self-important world leaders who had plunged Europe into a shockingly bloody and, in the minds of many Americans, unnecessary war.

For example, one night in 1917, Rogers drew his routine from Henry Ford's "peace ship," on which the automobile manufacturer had transported a team of prominent pacifists overseas to negotiate a swift end to the war. In the news story, he saw a chance to lampoon both Ford and Europe's heads of state:

Ford's all wrong, instead of taking a lot of them high-powered fellers on his ship, he should've hired away all these Ziegfeld pippins [show girls]. He'd not only get the boys out of the trenches by Christmas, but he'd have Kaiser Bill [Wilhelm II, the emperor of Germany] and Lloyd George [the prime minister of England] and Clemenceau [the premier of France] shootin' craps to see which one'd head the line at the stage door.

After the war's end, Rogers's most popular bits revealed his sympathy for the returning soldiers while also expressing his skepticism regarding the government's guarantees of future peace. In one show, he joked about the many parades staged for the veterans:

If we really wanted to honor our boys, why don't we let them sit on the reviewing stands and make the people march those 15 miles? They don't want to parade, they want to go home and rest. . . . If the money spent on stands and parades, and the high

A film still from Doubling for Romeo *(1920), a satire on the movie industry. Although Hollywood made Rogers an international celebrity, he enjoyed making fun of the town's supposed glitz and glamour.* (From the archives of the Will Rogers Memorial, Claremore, Oklahoma)

prices people paid for the seats, had been divided up amongst the soldiers they would have had enough to live comfortably on until the next war.

At the height of his career as a *Follies* star, Rogers fell into a new profession. In 1918, the movie producer Samuel Goldwyn hired him to act in a series of silent film comedies. He found the work unsatisfying. After perfecting his ability to deliver ad-libs at a rapid-fire pace to a live audience, he was frustrated just pantomiming scenarios written by someone else for nothing but a camera.

After starring in 13 films for Goldwyn, Rogers started his own movie company in 1921. Acting as a producer, director, writer, and star, he made three films. They were moderate successes, but they did not bring in enough money to keep him in business. Rogers then signed a two-year contract with Hal Roach, a legendary producer of slapstick comedy. Complaining that in Roach's movies all he did was "run around barns and lose my pants," Rogers fulfilled his obligation with little enthusiasm.

Weary of Hollywood, Rogers began concentrating on his burgeoning career as a newspaper columnist. Throughout most of the 1920s and the early 1930s, he wrote a weekly column and a short daily piece, which were syndicated in hundreds of newspapers across the United States. Essentially the print equivalent of his *Follies* act, they became Rogers's favorite forum for his political humor. Political parties, bankers, and Wall Street speculators were among his most popular targets.

But by the end of the 1920s, Rogers was focusing his comic observations on the instability of the American economy. While many experts were predicting prosperity for years to came, Rogers saw that the country was headed for disaster. In September 1928, he wrote:

No nation in the history of the world was ever sitting as pretty. If we want anything all we have to do is go and buy it on credit. So that leaves us without any economic problem whatever, except perhaps some day to have to pay for them. But we are certainly not thinking about that this early.

As Rogers had feared, the economy collapsed following the stock market crash of October 1929. Millions of Americans were suddenly impoverished and homeless. At first, the federal government was reluctant to help the newly poor. In many of his newspaper columns, Rogers expressed outrage toward the do-nothing approach of President Herbert Hoover and his administration. In one article, Rogers wrote:

> They seem to think that's a bad precedent, to appropriate money for food. It's too much like the "dole." They think it will encourage hunger. The way things look, hunger don't need much encouragement. It's just coming around naturally.

By the early 1930s, Rogers was the United States's most celebrated performer and political commentator. More than ever, the message behind his jokes was striking a nerve of ordinary Americans as they struggled with poverty. In his gentle way, he warned against trusting the government and big business—two forces that people were coming to blame for many of the hardships they were enduring.

Rogers claimed he inherited his sense of humor from his mother. But perhaps it was his politician father who had passed on to him a healthy suspicion of the powers that be. Certainly the mistreatment of the Cherokees by the U.S. government left a powerful impression on Rogers as a boy. It often became a subject for his humor, although his jokes about Cherokee history usually carried a bitter edge. For instance, in one column, he wrote about the United States's purchase of the Cherokee Strip, an oil-rich tract of land, for a mere dollar an acre:

> The Cherokee had a treaty that said: "You should have this land as long as the grass grows and water flows." It was not only a good rhyme, but it looked like a good treaty, and it was—til they struck oil. Then the government took it away from us again. They said, "The treaty only refers to 'water and grass'; it dident say anything about oil." So the Indians lost another bet. The first one to Andrew Jackson and the second to the oil companies.

Rogers's anger over the Cherokees' fate was not always so controlled. After his death, reporter Ben Dixon Mitchell recounted an incident that occurred during Rogers's 1928 lecture tour of North Carolina. On a visit to the Old Cherokee Nation, he performed before an audience of three thousand tribespeople. In the middle of his act, Rogers suddenly "became furious. . . . Some long-forgotten, in-bred memory welled up in his heart, and he ripped into Andrew Jackson." When he ended his diatribe, "Rogers stood, white, trembling, and actually aghast at himself. Afterward, he said wonderingly that he didn't know what had got into him."

During the depression, Rogers also renewed his film career. Starting in 1927, the movie industry had begun producing films with sound tracks. These "talkies" (or "noisies" as Rogers called them) proved an excellent medium to show off Rogers's talents. Unlike silents, in which he could only communicate through gestures, talkies allowed him to express himself verbally, thus take full advantage of the comic inflection and timing he had perfected on stage. However, he was rarely happy with the lines screenwriters prepared for him. Usually, he read them quickly to get a sense of what the film was about but improvised his dialogue while the camera was rolling.

His working habits infuriated his directors and fellow actors, but they produced movies that his fans loved. In 1935, Rogers was ranked as the second most popular star by the *Motion Picture Herald,* following only child star Shirley Temple. Despite his success, Rogers still disliked filmmaking. Each year, he hurriedly produced three movies in six months so that for at least half his time he would be free to "have fun without some director hollering at me."

Traveling was Rogers's favorite way to spend his time off. He had already taken three trips around the globe when, in the summer of 1935, aviation pioneer Wiley Post invited Rogers to join him on a flight to Alaska and Siberia. He jumped at the opportunity. Rogers was particularly eager to see Siberia again. Years before, he had taken a train through the region and was struck by how much its unspoiled countryside reminded him of the Indian Territory of his youth.

On August 15, 1935, Post's plane crashed into a frozen lagoon outside the town of Barrow, Alaska. Both the pilot and his passenger were killed instantly. The next day, the deaths of Will Rogers and Wiley Post were front-page news all over the world. Rogers certainly had been one of the most famous performers of his day, but even for a celebrity of his stature, the outpouring of emotion that followed was incredible. For weeks, newspapers devoted pages to memories of Rogers. His wife, Betty, received thousands of letters of condolence, and Congress halted its deliberations to pay a special tribute to its longtime critic. On August 22, more than 50 thousand mourners traveled to Los Angeles to attend his funeral. Most had never met Rogers, but they grieved as though they had lost a close friend.

◆ ◆ ◆

Since Rogers's death, few performers have had such an impact on the American public. His versatility in part explains his influence. During his more than 30 years in show business, popular entertainment was constantly changing. When vaudeville was replaced by silent films and silents were replaced by talkies, many performers saw their careers end. Rogers, however, was amazingly adept at finding the way of changing his act in order to showcase best his unusual talents in any medium.

Rogers's popularity also owed much to the persona he developed early in his career. Exaggerating rural speech, appearance, and manners, Rogers, through his stage character, could speak freely, making comments and criticisms that might have offended his audience if they were spoken by a more forceful or sophisticated figure. As his *Follies* costar W. C. Fields noted with envy, "[Rogers] can get away with anything."

Rogers's cowboy image held a special appeal as well. In the early 20th century, many Americans, especially Easterners in urban areas, had a romanticized view of cowboys. To them, cowboys represented freedom and independence, both of which were becoming increasingly scarce in the lives of workers in the industrialized United States. To some extent, Rogers's Indian heritage had a similar meaning. Although western movies propagated stereotypes by depicting Indians as savages, they also idealized traditional Indian life as an enviably simple and burden-free existence.

With his candor about the United States's persecution of the Cherokees, Rogers offered his audiences a much different vision of Indian life. His view was confirmed by the 1928 government study know as the Meriam Report, which revealed that U.S. policy had made Indians the poorest minority in the country. During an era in which many white Americans developed a contempt for the government, these revelations made some see Indians in a new light. Rather than viewing Indians as enemies or merely curiosities, they imagined them as noble underdogs in a centuries-long fight against insensitive authorities. Long condemned for their "foreign" ways, Indians now seemed the quintessential Americans. Rogers could then be seen as, in the words of a reviewer for the *New York Times*, "an American from the grass roots—the most American of present-day comedians, in fact, since through his veins there courses authentic Cherokee Indian blood." In this way, Rogers's Indianness helped to make him into an American folk hero.

Rogers's image as an Indian cowboy, of course, would have much less impact if it had not been genuine. Likewise, his pose as "just an old country boy" would have felt false if it had not been rooted in his upbringing. Rogers may have traveled the world and associated with kings and presidents, but, true to his presentation of himself, he was still and always a product of the rural West.

Rogers himself saw honesty as the key to his appeal. He once explained his comic style with, "I use only one set method in my little gags, and that is to try to keep to the truth. Of course you can exaggerate it, but what you say must be based on truth." To many Americans during the Great Depression, such veracity seemed rare. Feeling betrayed and abandoned by politicians and other public figures, they relied on Rogers to have the courage to tell them the truth and the kindness to temper it with humor.

IRON EYES CODY

◆ ◆ ◆

Cherokee-Cree Film Actor
(1904–   )

Dressed in buckskin finery, an Indian man paddles a canoe up to a riverbank. He climbs out onto dry land by a highway swarming with cars. For a moment, he pauses to watch the traffic pass. As one car speeds by, a passenger tosses from his window a bundle of trash, which falls at the Indian's feet.

The Indian glances at the trash, then slowly raises his face, and looks unblinkingly into the camera. His stony features fill the screen, but betray no emotion. The single tear rolling down his cheek, however, eloquently conveys his horror at seeing his beautiful homeland defiled by the motorist's thoughtless act.

First telecast in 1970, the image of the crying Indian since has been seen in nearly 15 billion homes. According to the Ad Council, the television spot, sponsored by Keep America Beautiful, is one of the most successful television public service announcements ever produced. Since its initial airing, the ad has cautioned several generations against careless desecration of the planet and its resources.

It has also made the face of Iron Eyes Cody recognizable to audiences around the world. But, as devotees of movie and television westerns well know, Cody's fame hardly came overnight. It followed a decades-long career spent in front of and behind the

This close-up of Iron Eyes Cody concluded an extremely popular public service announcement produced by the environmental organization Keep America Beautiful in 1970. This image made Cody's face famous throughout the world. (Keep America Beautiful, Inc.)

camera. Involved in the making of more than two hundred movies, Cody is perhaps the most prolific of all Indian actors in Hollywood's history.

◆ ◆ ◆

Born on April 3, 1904, Oscar Cody grew up on a ranch in the Cherokee Nation in what is now Oklahoma. Until about 80 years before his birth, Cody's ancestors had lived in the Cherokees' homeland in the southeastern United States. In 1838, his paternal great-grandfather, along with most of the Cherokee people, had been forced to migrate west by the U.S. government, which then opened the tribe's ancestral territory for settlement by white Americans. During the long and difficult journey, now known as the Trail of Tears, thousands of the Cherokee travelers died.

As the Cherokees set about rebuilding their nation in an unfamiliar land, the tribe entered one of the bleakest periods of its history, marked by political in-fighting, assassination, and the constant threat of civil war. Growing up amid this turmoil, Cody's grandfather, Randolf Abshire Codey, took up horse stealing as a profession. He eventually amassed enough cash and horses to establish his own ranch.

His son, Thomas Longplume Codey, inherited Randolf's criminal bent along with the family business. Tom increased his stock by posing as a horse veterinarian to local farmers. He often exaggerated the ailments of the animals he treated in order to trick their owners into selling them at a bargain price. Codey also made his living by performing in Buffalo Bill's Wild West Show, a popular traveling exhibition of trick riding, sharpshooting, and historical pageants. While working for William "Buffalo Bill" Cody, Tom decided to drop the "e" from his surname in the hope of capturing for himself some of the famed showman's allure.

During the show's tours, Tom Cody traveled throughout the American West. At each stop, he bought up clothing, pottery, baskets, and other creations made by local Indian artisans. During visits home, Cody exhibited these while lecturing to paying audiences about Indian lore.

Occasionally, Tom took the time to share with Oscar his extensive knowledge of Indian legends and languages. More often, however, he was a distant parent, prone to drunken binges and violence. Despite his erratic behavior and long absences, Oscar's mother, Frances, a woman of Cree Indian ancestry, maintained a structured and solid home for the boy and his eight brothers and sisters, most of whom were abandoned Indian children whom his mother had adopted.

When Oscar Cody was a teenager, two men from Hollywood arrived at the family's doorstep. They were scouting locations for a silent movie titled *Back to God's Country*. An epic about the Civil War, the film was to include a long sequence during which several soldiers were hiding out in a cornfield. The scouts asked to rent the large field adjoining the Cody's ranch for the filming.

Soon, the ranch was swarming with cameramen, actors, and extras. Oscar was entranced by the energy expended on making the movie; his father was more excited by the rent money he was able to coax out of Irvin Willet, the film's director. Both Codys were eager to take Willet's advice that they seek their fortunes in Hollywood. According to the director, the film industry had plenty of jobs for Indians.

At that time, nearly one out of every five American movies made was a western. The success of the genre was due in large part to the popularity of Wild West shows. In imitation of these spectacles, the climax of many early film westerns was a reenactment of a historical battle between Indians and U.S. soldiers. Western filmmakers were eager to hire actual Indians to play warriors in such scenes. Unlike most non-Indian actors, many Indian extras could supply their own costumes, could ride horses well, and were willing to accept low wages because so few other jobs were open to them.

Accompanied by Oscar, Tom Cody moved to Los Angeles and quickly found regular work as a technical adviser for movie westerns. He was responsible for teaching non-Indian actors playing Indians just enough about Indian sign language and dances to make their performances seem authentic to moviegoers. As a lucrative sideline, Cody also rented out his collection of Indian clothing and artifacts to costume designers and prop managers.

A bit part in *Back to God's Country* had persuaded Oscar to pursue a career in acting. Using the stage name "Iron Eyes," he found occasional acting jobs, but he spent most of his time helping his father, who was often too drunk to perform his duties. Iron Eyes's first major venture into technical advising was on the set of *The Covered Wagon* (1923), which was the most expensive western made to date. In addition to acting in the film, Iron Eyes helped his father manage and direct the five hundred Sioux and Arapaho extras.

The success of *The Covered Wagon* spawned a series of imitations, which in turn created a great demand for Iron Eyes's proven ability to handle an enormous company of actors. However, throughout the 1930s, he worked most often on "Bs"—inexpensively produced, formulaic movies that were shown as the second halves of double features. Aside from providing technical advice, he offered his clients access to an archive of more than 50,000 feet of filmed Indian battles, which he had collected during his first years in Hollywood. Working with shoestring budgets, many "B" western producers were eager to buy his stock footage to avoid the expense of shooting action scenes themselves.

The rise of the "Bs" created more work than ever for Indian extras. Nevertheless, Cody had no difficulty finding people willing to take on the low-paying jobs. Many impoverished Indians, hard hit by the Great Depression, flocked to Los Angeles in search of work. At bars, on breadlines, and among the crews of government construction projects, Cody discovered all the actors he needed.

After hiring the extras, Cody functioned as their acting coach. Most westerns were set in the Great Plains, but his actors were of tribes from all over the United States. For those completely unfamiliar with Plains culture, Cody provided clothing and some language instruction so that they could fake the sound of Plains Indian words if their parts demanded that they speak.

However, even the Plains Indians he recruited required some instruction. Cody had to teach them to behave like "movie Indians." As depicted in most westerns, Indians were wild, whooping, bloodthirsty villains whose persecution of settlers or soldiers was used as a convenient device to propel the plot or an excuse for a gratuitous action scene. Even in films based on specific historical events, the Indians' reasons for attacking settlers were rarely explored. Rather than depicting Indians as human beings defending their homes, they were largely shown as savages for whom the murder of innocent whites was a form of entertainment.

In their treatment on the set, Indian actors also were granted little respect by most filmmakers and movie companies. Cody's autobiography relates one incident that occurred while he was working as an adviser for veteran director Cecil B. DeMille on *The Plainsman* (1936). During the filming, Cody supervised 2,500 Sioux and Cheyenne extras, whose wage of $15 a day was "a small fortune for these people." The movie's battle scenes, which Cody helped direct, were to be shot in Montana. Almost as soon as the cast and crew arrived on the filming site, a snowstorm swept in and blocked the transportation routes into and out of the movie set. Stranded for weeks with a limited supply of food, the Indian extras were doled out starvation rations, while the non-Indian employees were allowed to eat whatever they wanted. The Indians' resentment toward this inequality nearly triggered a riot before the storm lifted and filming resumed.

Despite this bitter experience, Cody welcomed the chance to work with DeMille again on *Union Pacific* (1939). His contribution to this film earned him a four-year contract with the director. In the same year, Cody acted as a technical consultant for *Stagecoach.* This western classic made a star of John Wayne, a longtime friend of Cody's, and revived the major studios' flagging interest in the genre.

In addition to drawing on bigger budgets, westerns in the 1940s began exploring new subjects. In the past, western films had owed much of their popularity to their simplicity and predictability. Especially among the "Bs," plots varied little; audiences could count on a story in which good, symbolized by noble lawmen or settlers, would conquer evil, usually represented by Indian warriors. In breaking away from the restrictions and simplemindedness of these stories, the new breed of westerns presented characters with far more psychological complexity.

The portrayal of Indians was particularly affected by this trend. In the late 1940s and early 1950s, many westerns focused attention on the personalities and motivations of Indian characters. To a certain extent, these parts reflected the respect some Americans had developed for the Indians because of the distinguished service of Indian soldiers in World War II (1939–45). Many filmmakers also found that the more balanced depictions helped them tell the stories that interested them most. The turmoil of the war had inspired many artists to reexamine American society and its values. Westerns provided filmmakers with a forum for discussing issues concerning law, government, and justice that might have been deemed as too controversial if they were dealt with in a film with a contemporary setting. Likewise, stories about Indian and white relations attracted directors and screenwriters who wanted to comment indirectly on American race relations in general.

The most acclaimed of these movies was *Broken Arrow* (1950), which told the story of the friendship between the great Apache

Playing the role of Tesse, Cody stands behind James Stewart in this still from Broken Arrow (1950), *a landmark in the depiction of Indians on screen. In this scene, considered highly controversial in its day, Stewart's character marries an Indian woman.* (Courtesy of the Museum of Modern Art Film Stills Archive)

leader Cochise and the white adventurer Thomas Jeffords. The movie not only took a sympathetic view of Cochise's battle with the U.S. Army to protect the Apache homeland, but also featured Indian actors in important roles. Following past tradition, Cochise was played by a white leading man, Jeff Chandler; however, the substantial part of Geronimo was played by Mohawk actor Jay Silverheels, who later gained fame as Tonto on the "Lone Ranger" television show. Cody appeared in the lesser, but significant, role of Cochise's friend Tesse. The high visibility of this part was a boon to his acting career. It helped win him notable roles in westerns throughout the 1950s, such as *Sitting Bull* (1954), *Broken Lance* (1954), and *Run of the Arrow* (1957).

Cody also found success in the new medium of television. In the late 1940s, he began hosting a local show in Los Angeles with his wife Birdie. The couple had met in 1922 on the set of *The Scarlet*

Letter, in which both appeared. Birdie Cody eventually left show business and became a noted archaeologist and assistant at the renowned Southwest Museum. Drawing on Birdie's expertise and Iron Eyes's showmanship, "Iron Eyes' Adventure" sought to instruct a non-Indian audience about Native American history and customs.

One of the show's fans was movie producer and theme park entrepreneur Walt Disney. He hired Cody to star in "The First Americans," a television show that the actor felt provided an accurate depiction of Indian life. Because of the show's success, Cody became a favorite player in Disney movies and television shows for many years. He also frequently landed guest spots on series, such as "Gunsmoke" and "Branded," which offered older, loyal westerns fans the same type of simple stories that the "Bs" had in the past.

In the late 1960s, Hollywood shied away from the western genre. At that time, activists for Native American rights were loudly attacking the film industry for its propagation of Indian stereotypes. In time, however, some moviemakers responded to their complaints with films about Indian peoples that attempted to tell their stories from an Indian perspective.

Among these films were two that Cody counts, along with *Broken Arrow,* as the most accurate portrayals of Indians in which he has acted. *A Man Called Horse* (1970) depicted the everyday lives of a group of Sioux Indians in 1820 as witnessed by a white man they had taken captive. Based on a Cheyenne legend, *Grayeagle* (1977) similarly was about a white mountain man's experiences with Indians in the early 19th century.

While Cody was on the set of *A Man Called Horse,* a representative from an advertising agency approached him with an invitation to appear in a public service announcement for Keep America Beautiful. Founded in 1953, the organization is dedicated to reducing litter by creating recycling programs and improved methods for handling waste. A longtime advocate of conservation, Cody eagerly agreed to appear in the spot, which eventually made his image a symbol of environmental awareness around the world.

Following the death of his wife in 1977, Cody decided to curtail his acting career in order to devote himself to charity work. In addition to lecturing to reservation youth groups about the dangers of alcohol abuse, he donates much of his time to the Los Angeles Native American Indian Commission, the Boy Scouts of America, and the Southwest Museum. He also remains involved with two organizations that he helped to found—the Los Angeles Indian Center, a 40-year-old institution that offers aid and counseling to Indian residents of the city, and the Little Big Horn Association, a nationwide service club that promotes the study of Indian cultures.

◆ ◆ ◆

A veteran of more than 50 years in the movie industry, Cody and his career reveal how the image of Indians on film has changed over time. In the earliest silent westerns, the technical limitations of the medium restricted any attempts at characterization. But by the late 1920s, when sound movies were introduced and films became feature length, the gulf between the depiction of non-Indians and Indians in westerns widened. Non-Indians were often rounded characters with whom the audience could sympathize; Indians, however, remained grunting primitives.

As Cody explains in his autobiography, working in films that promoted Indian stereotypes was discomforting to him and his fellow Indian actors. But their control over their characters was small; Indian players either did as they were told or they did not work. Nevertheless, as Cody points out, Indian film performers did achieve certain personal gains through their work: "The Indians we hired as extras were . . . swept along with the joy of being paid decently at something which was, really, a lot of fun: riding horses, shooting, and yelling."

Beginning in the 1950s, the movie industry and its audiences had matured enough to allow for a slightly more realistic view of Indians. Because of his power in Hollywood, Cody was in a position to take advantage of the situation. After the filming of *Broken Arrow*, Cody's popularity gave him the luxury to choose roles carefully and to reject lines and direction that he deemed inaccurate and inappropriate. Many younger Indian actors have since carried on his efforts to gain respect for Indians and Indian culture within the movie business. The fight continues, but as rich and multi-faceted roles for Indians become more commonplace, the battle may prove to be one of the few ever won by Indians in Hollywood.

MARIA TALLCHIEF

◆ ◆ ◆

Osage Ballerina
(1925–   )

In the dark theater, the audience sat silently, eager for the ballet
to begin. Just as their patience had begun to fray, the orchestra
sounded its first notes, filling the auditorium with deep and
ominous tones. The curtain then slowly rose to reveal a beautiful, ghostly painting depicting the firebird of Russian folk legend. The crowd responded with a smattering of clapping,
which grew louder as the young man playing the role of the
prince danced across the stage and exited as a spotlight moved
over the backdrop. Suddenly into the amber beam flew another
dancer, a ballerina wearing a crest of plumes and a flaming red
costume that, sprinkled with gold dust, glittered in the light.
First awed by her appearance, the audience soon was transfixed
by the ballerina's movements. Highly controlled yet filled with
passionate intensity, they made the dancer seem as supernatural
as the magical firebird of myth.

Hours later, when the curtain fell, the auditorium was filled
with the sound of applause and shouts of "bravo." While the
audience rose to its feet for an ovation, the choreographer
emerged from backstage. A moment later, the ballerina walked
out to join him and, in her first awkward movement of the
evening, stumbled forward and nervously took her bows. The

Maria Tallchief strikes a pose from Firebird *(1949), the ballet that made her a star both in the United States and Europe.* (The Dance Collection, The New York Public Library for the Performing Arts, Astor, Lenox and Tilden Foundations)

crowd then thundered out a new cheer—"Tallchief, Tallchief, Tallchief."

For the young ballerina, Maria Tallchief, the applause was only beginning. Reviewers of the premiere of *Firebird* on November 27, 1949, hailed her performance with enthusiasm and predicted for her a glorious future. One critic praised her "almost frightening technical range." Another claimed she "was truly an amazing figure—she preened, she shimmered, she gloried in speed and airy freedom." All agreed that she was something new in the world of ballet: Tallchief was the first American-born dancer to emerge as a superstar.

◆ ◆ ◆

Twenty-four years earlier, on January 24, 1925, Elizabeth Marie Tallchief (known as Betty Marie to her family) was born in Fairfax, Oklahoma, a small town located on the Osage Indian Reservation. Traditionally, the Osage Indians had occupied a vast territory, including portions of present-day Missouri, Arkansas, Kansas, and Oklahoma. In the 17th century, French explorers visited the tribe and claimed their homeland for France, which in turn sold the area to the United States in 1803 as part of the Louisiana Purchase. Initially, the Osages resisted the flood of American settlers who soon invaded their lands. However, as the settlers' numbers increased, the tribe's leadership felt compelled to cede portions of their land to the U.S. government in order to keep the peace. Instrumental in these dealings during the mid-19th century was Chief Peter Big Heart, Tallchief's paternal great-grandfather. As one of the few Osages who spoke English, Big Heart acted as an interpreter during the negotiation of several important treaties.

By 1870, the Osages' territory had been reduced to a tract in what is now northeastern Oklahoma. Like most Indian groups confined to reservations during that era, the Osages initially had difficulty making a living and maintaining their traditional ways while restricted to a relatively small patch of land. However, the fortunes of the tribespeople changed suddenly in 1897 when the reservation was found to be resting atop a huge pool of oil. By leasing their oil-rich tracts to petroleum drilling companies in exchange for a percentage of the profits, the Osage people grew very wealthy very quickly. Throughout the first few decades of the 20th century, several Osages were ranked among the richest people in the United States.

Although not the wealthiest on the reservation, Tallchief's family was certainly affluent. Her father used his oil royalties to buy real estate. These investments yielded enough profit to support the Tallchiefs in a life of leisure. Easygoing by nature, Tallchief's father, Alexander, filled his days with golf games and visits to Fairfax's movie theater and pool hall, both of which he owned. Her mother, Ruth, however, was uncomfortable with too much idle time. A strict woman of Dutch, Scottish, and Irish descent, she was determined to pass along to her children her own respect for the character-building merits of hard work and sacrifice.

When Tallchief and her younger sister, Marjorie, were still toddlers, Ruth began training them to be well-rounded ladies with a regimen of lessons in music and dance. Both daughters immediately showed promise in the arts, but Betty Marie was by far the more determined in her efforts to earn her mother's praise by excelling in class. By the age of four, she was dancing in toe shoes and playing simple pieces on the piano.

When Betty Marie was seven, the Tallchiefs moved to Los Angeles, California, so that the girls could study with the best teachers available. As soon as the family was settled in Beverly Hills, Betty Marie and Marjorie were signed up for classes with ballet master Ernest Belcher, who immediately insisted that they forget all the showy steps they had learned from their amateur instructors in Fairfax. Under Belcher's tutelage, Betty Marie and Marjorie developed a solid base in ballet's fundamentals and began to perform before paying audiences. In their repertoire was an "Indian" dance that the girls performed wearing buckskin skirts and headdresses. The dance and costumes, both conceived by their teacher, were in no way authentic. Betty Marie and Marjorie's only knowledge of actual Indian dance was from dim memories of witnessing Osage ceremonies as very small children.

In her teens, Betty Marie enrolled in the dancing school of Bronislava Nijinska, a Russian ballerina and choreographer whose world-famous brother, Vaslav Nijinski, was considered one of the greatest dancers of his day. Betty Marie was quickly drawn to Nijinska, a sophisticated woman who counted several Hollywood celebrities as close friends. Nijinska was also an inspired teacher who expected her students to approach ballet with complete devotion and carry themselves with utmost dignity both inside and outside of the classroom. Because of Nijinska's influence, Betty Marie lost enthusiasm for her piano lessons and made plans for a career in ballet.

After graduating from Beverly Hills High School in 1942, Betty Marie Tallchief set off for New York City. There she landed a job with the Canadian touring troupe of the Ballet Russe de Monte Carlo, then the world's most famous ballet company. The thrill of becoming a professional dancer was colored by the cold reception she received by the other company members. When the dancers learned she was an Osage, they assumed her family had used oil money to buy her a place in the Ballet Russe. Soon enough, however, Tallchief's obvious talents dispelled the rumors that she did not earn her position.

After the tour, Tallchief was asked to join the Ballet Russe permanently as a member of the *corps de ballet,* the troupe of young dancers who supported the soloists. With the new job, she was expected to take on a stage name—Maria Tallchieva. In order to maintain its glamorous reputation and international cache, the company encouraged its dancers to Russianize their names. Though usually compliant, Tallchief in this case firmly rejected her instructors' advice. To her "Tallchieva" sounded undignified. As a compromise, however, she agreed to drop "Betty Marie" and adopt "Maria" in its place.

Maria Tallchief proved to be an unusually diligent student during the company's rehearsals. On her own time, she also took extra classes at the recently formed School of the American Ballet. So that she would be ready to take a lead if asked, Tallchief also learned all of the roles in the Ballet Russe's repertoire.

Her chance came in May 1943, when she filled in for an injured soloist in the *Chopin Concerto,* a ballet choreographed by her old teacher Nijinska. For two weeks, Tallchief danced the part to great acclaim. The Ballet Russe's publicists rushed to capitalize on her new celebrity by touting her as the "beautiful dancing Osage" in the belief that her audiences would find her Indian ancestry exotic. Tallchief herself found the publicity embarrassing. Hounded by the publicists for stories about growing up as an Indian, Tallchief explained that she could not think of any. In fact, her childhood had resembled those of the wealthy patrons of the ballet more than of most other Indian people.

In 1944, Tallchief became the student of George Balanchine, the Russian-born choreographer and cofounder of the School of American Ballet, when he was asked to join the Ballet Russe as its ballet master. Known for favoring promising young ballerinas over more experienced dancers, Balanchine immediately spotted Tallchief's potential. Her long legs and straight back epitomized the body type that he felt was ideal for a dancer. Her olive skin and high cheekbones gave her face the same dignity that he admired in those of the legendary Russian ballerinas. Her training as a pianist afforded her a knowledge of music and sense of timing that Balanchine rarely found in dancers. Most compelling of all, however, was her dedication. He was awed by Tallchief's devotion to ballet and her willingness to give herself over entirely to a teacher whom she trusted.

In reward for her commitment to her art and his instruction, Balanchine gave Tallchief lead parts in *Danses Concertantes* (1944) and *La Somnambuliste* (*Night Shadow*, 1946). He also created her most complex role to date in *Le Baiser de la Fée* (*The Kiss of the Fairy*, 1946), which was based on Hans Christian Andersen's fairy tale "The Ice Queen." In Balanchine's interpretation, Tallchief danced the dual role of an ethereal fairy queen and of an earthy gypsy women. Several dance critics admired her skill at conveying this broad emotional range.

To the surprise of the dance world, Tallchief and Balanchine were married on August 16, 1946. Balanchine was more than twice her age and, before the wedding, had displayed no more warmth toward her than toward his other dancers. The 20-year-old Tallchief herself was caught off guard by his proposal. As she recounted in the 1989 television documentary "Dancing for Mr. B," "When we were married, it was almost really like I was the material he wanted to use. . . . By this time, he knew he wanted to start [a] company, and I think he knew that here was the beginning of a company."

Indeed Balanchine soon set off on his own by cofounding the Ballet Society. At the newly opened New York City Center, the dancers of the Ballet Society performed under his direction for a small audience of devoted fans. Unlike the Ballet Russe and its rival Ballet Theater, which appealed to the growing number of regular theatergoers drawn to classical dance, the Ballet Society catered to a tiny elite interested in the newest and most innovative productions.

In the spring of 1947, Tallchief accompanied Balanchine to France, where he served as a guest director at the Paris Opera for a season. She herself was asked to join the Paris Opera as a guest artist, thereby becoming the first American ballerina to perform on its stage in 108 years. Paris reporters were fascinated by the young dancer and as eager as their American counterparts to fabricate stories about her Indian heritage. Noting the sense of majesty in her stage demeanor, some writers claimed Tallchief was an "Indian princess," becoming the first of the many European reporters who would embroider tales about her youth to appeal to their readers' interest in royalty. Convinced that no American could dance ballet with the skill and confidence of Tallchief, a few other reviewers spread a rumor that she was actually of French and Russian descent but that she had been given an Indian surname by the company to make her seem more American.

After returning home from France, Tallchief joined the Ballet Society, which was soon renamed the New York City Ballet. Many of her fans were stunned that she chose to give up her career with the Ballet Russe to dance for her husband's new and untried company. Despite the rumors that Tallchief had committed career suicide, she had no doubts about devoting herself to becoming the leading Balanchine dancer. Tallchief recognized her husband's genius both as a choreographer and as a teacher. As she explained in a 1989 portrait in *Interview* magazine, "I was in the right place and I knew it. I worked hard as I could to be able to dance the way I knew George wanted me to dance."

In the New York City Ballet's first few seasons, Tallchief drew raves for her performances in *The Four Temperaments* (1946), *Symphonie Concertante* (1947), and *Orpheus* (1948). Balanchine adapted her roles to showcase her greatest talents as a dancer: her speed, her strength, her stamina, and her faultless technique. In 1949, he decided to create his own version of *Firebird*, a classic Russian ballet, with the title role tailored especially for Tallchief. Incorporating all the steps she had performed best in class, he choreographed her role in four days. Although Tallchief knew each individual step well, she was daunted by the part he crafted, which called for her to perform these movements in rapid-fire succession.

After weeks of diligent practice, Tallchief had mastered the difficult part, which she performed flawlessly at the ballet's premiere. In the many enthusiastic reviews, the first performance of *Firebird* was declared a landmark, an assessment that dance historians have since corroborated. The debut signaled the beginnings of the shift of the center of the dance world from Paris to New York City, and more specifically to the New York City Ballet. As the company's leading ballerina, Tallchief had begun her tenure as an international star.

Reviewers and fans continued to lavish praise on the New York City Ballet through its next few seasons, although some writers began to complain that Balanchine's technically perfect dancers seemed unemotional and passionless. By some, Tallchief was dismissed as one of Balanchine's "Frigidaire ballerinas," especially after her relatively lackluster interpretation of the fiery siren in *The Prodigal Son* (1950) and unconvincing portrayal as a fun-loving teenage beachcomber in *Jones Beach* (1950).

Even more disturbing for Tallchief than lukewarm reviews were the pressure of being both Balanchine's lead dancer and his wife. Balanchine was extremely hard on his favored dancers, constantly challenging them to perform increasingly more difficult steps, always faster and with more precision. The stress on Tallchief was particularly great because, as the company's *prima ballerina*, her technique was expected to set the style and tone of all of the dancers' performances. Tallchief eventually found the fatigue of trying to please Balanchine at the studio and at home overwhelming. In 1950, the couple separated, and the following spring their marriage was annulled. Neither Tallchief nor Balanchine wanted to sever their close professional ties, however. The day their annulment became legal, Tallchief arrived at the studio on schedule, signaling to the rest of the company that the work relationship between she and her mentor was to continue unchanged.

The end of Tallchief's marriage to Balanchine, in some sense, actually proved beneficial to her career. Relieved of the burden of Balanchine's constant attention, she felt freer as an artist and less timid as a performer. The new roles Balanchine created for her, in ballets such as *Serenade* (1952) and *Scotch Symphony* (1952) and in his versions of *Swan Lake* (1951) and *The Nutcracker* (1954), took full advantage of her new aura of maturity and authority.

In 1953, Tallchief's international success was celebrated by the Osage Tribal Council, the governing body of the Osage Nation. In recognition of the distinction she had brought to the Osage people, she was named Princess Wa-Txthe-thonba, meaning "the Woman of Two Standards." The purely honorary title acknowledged her importance in both the Osage community and the world beyond. The Oklahoma State Senate further honored her by declaring June 29, 1953, Maria Tallchief Day.

In 1954, Tallchief briefly left the New York City Ballet to rejoin the Ballet Russe, which needed her star power to launch its international tour. Throughout Europe, Tallchief had become a top box office draw and developed a reputation as the only living dancer who could rival in technical mastery the greatest European and Russian ballerinas. To lure her back, the Ballet Russe had offered her the extraordinarily high salary of $2,000 a week. In the cover story of its October 11, 1954 issue, *Newsweek* declared that Tallchief was then the highest paid ballerina in the world.

After a season filled with injuries and creative disappointments, Tallchief left the Ballet Russe and returned to the New York City Ballet, where she remained for the rest of her dancing career. Although for the next 10 years she remained the most prominently featured ballerina in the company, the attention Balanchine gave

Maria Tallchief (center) at a 1991 ceremony at the Oklahoma State Capitol
held to dedicate a mural of five renowned Indian ballerinas from the state.
The other honored dancers are Yvonne Chouteau (Cherokee), Rosella
Hightower (Choctaw), Maria's sister Marjorie Tallchief (Osage), and
Moscelyne Larkin (Shawnee). (Photo courtesy of the State Arts Council
of Oklahoma)

to young and less experienced dancers increasingly frustrated Tallchief. She also grew weary of commuting to New York from Chicago, where she lived with Henry "Buzz" Paschen, Jr., a construction company executive, whom she married in 1956. The constant travel became even more straining after the birth of her daughter, Elisa, in 1959. In 1965, at age 40, Tallchief announced that she was retiring as a dancer in order to spend more time with her family.

Nine years later, Tallchief was drawn back into the dance world at the request of the Lyric Opera of Chicago, which asked her to train its singers to enter and exit the stage gracefully. Soon Tallchief's Ballet School of the Lyric Opera developed its own corps of dancers and began touring throughout the Midwest. With the encouragement of Balanchine, Tallchief severed her relationship with the Lyric Opera and established the Chicago City Ballet in 1980. Affiliated with the School of the American Ballet, the 20-member company concentrated on Balanchine's major works, which Tallchief trained her dancers to perform in the "Balanchine style." Especially after Balanchine's death in 1983, Tallchief devoted herself to preserving his teaching methods and became openly critical of other companies who simplified Balanchine's original choreography to eliminate steps that their ballerinas deemed too challenging. Due to a lack of funding, the Chicago City Ballet was disbanded in 1989; however, Tallchief remains a powerful force in the ballet world and a leading advocate for the proper performance of Balanchine's works.

◆ ◆ ◆

Like that of any other creative artist, Maria Tallchief's career has been shaped in part by the time in which she has lived. Despite her skill, in another era she might not have enjoyed the same success. Before the onset of World War II (1939–45), few Americans had access to the training and education needed to become master performers in older European-based arts, such as ballet, opera, and classical music. However, during and especially after the war, many talented foreign immigrants, such as George Balanchine, flocked to the United States to escape the turmoil in their native countries. Promising young American students, such as Maria Tallchief, eagerly absorbed their expertise and, in the process, brought an invigorating new American perspective and energy to Old World arts. As a result, in the years following the war, the United States emerged as, not only a major world political power, but also as a center for international culture.

The amount and type of media attention Maria Tallchief received was fueled largely by Americans' pride in their new pre-eminence in the arts. As reporters rarely failed to mention, Tallchief was not only American born, but also a *Native* American. Characteristic of the publicity surrounding Tallchief, *Time* magazine raved after the premiere of *Firebird:* "Onstage, Maria looks as regal and exotic as a Russian princess; offstage, she is as American as wampum and apple pie." This view of Indianness, as an exaggerated form of Americanness, contrasted the perception of Indians as "foreigners" with odd values and beliefs that were still held by many non-Indians.

For the most part, however, the attention paid to Tallchief's heritage at the height of her dancing career revealed how little prevailing attitudes toward Indians had changed. In the eyes of some reviewers and reporters, especially those in Europe, Tallchief's ancestry had imbued her with both a special dignity and a rawness—claims that drew shamelessly on the centuries-old stereotype of the Indian as a "noble savage." More commonly, writers merely discussed her Indianness with a slightly mocking tone that communicated both an ignorance of and disrespect for Indian cultures.

Throughout her career, Tallchief herself has avoided drawing connections between her Indianness and her work as a dancer. As her relative silence on the subject implies, her Indian heritage has, in fact, had little direct influence on her career or success. Her triumphs, however, have had an influence on non-Indians' perceptions of Indian people. In the 1950s, journalists felt free to present the concept of an Indian ballerina as peculiar, even comic. The notion underlying such ridicule—the idea that Native Americans possess an innate savagery that renders them unable to appreciate high culture—since has been recognized almost universally as both absurd and racist, in part because of the example of Tallchief. Throughout her career, she has effectively countered stereotypes, not with words, but with her quiet dignity and, most of all, her immense talent.

BUFFY SAINTE-MARIE

◆ ◆ ◆

Cree Singer-Songwriter
(1942–   )

In the middle of the stage was a young woman, little more than 20 years old, half sitting on a wooden stool with an acoustic guitar on her lap. A few people in the audience had arrived early enough to get table seats, but most had to stand, wedged close and into every corner, jostling one another to get a better view of the singer. With nothing but her guitar, her trembling voice, and her passion, she had enthralled the crowd for hours.

The audience now understood why she had been hailed as the latest folk sensation, but some were still surprised by her appearance. The other singers on the coffeehouse circuit shunned costumes and makeup. To show they were above the trappings of the world of mainstream entertainment, they wore all black or arrived on stage in the same jeans or khakis they had put on that morning. This singer, however, saw no shame in theatricality. Her waist-length, raven black hair, her sharp features, and bright red, cobra-skin dress announced that she was not like everyone else, that she was a performer with a unique gift and eager to share it with whomever would listen.

Many of her songs were about love, especially of its passing. These she sang in a low, sad voice. Others told stories of anger and rage, the words to which she sometimes growled or even yelled out to drive their point home. One such song, "My Country 'Tis of Thy People You're Dying," chronicled the United States's long and horrific abuse of Native Americans. As the singer struck its final chords, the audience gave her an enthusiastic round of applause.

The reaction was familiar. In many other clubs, she had sung this indictment of white injustice to a crowd of non-Indians and felt just as uncomfortable hearing their clapping and cheers as she did this night. To quiet them and hopefully to make them reflect on what she had sung, she repeated, through a sly smile, the response she had developed for such occasions: "I hope you're offended."

During her 30-year career, Buffy Sainte-Marie has often aimed to offend. Unafraid of anger but terrified of complacency, she has used her considerable talents to provoke her audiences to think about political issues, particularly the plight of Native Americans in the past and, more important, in the present. Sainte-Marie has undoubtedly succeeded in offending some listeners, but she has inspired many more to reexamine their prejudices and their sense of history and, as a result, to work toward affecting social change.

◆ ◆ ◆

Beverly Sainte-Marie was born on February 20, 1942, on the Piapot Reserve in the Canadian province of Saskatchewan, the home of one branch of the Cree Indians. When she was only several months old, her parents died suddenly and a church group took over her care. Without the consent of her Cree relations, the church arranged for her adoption by a Wakefield, Massachusetts couple, Albert and Winifred Sainte-Marie, who nicknamed the girl "Buffy." Although her adoptive mother was part Micmac Indian, her upbringing was identical to that of any white child reared in this Boston suburb.

As a girl, Buffy was withdrawn and unsociable. She shied away from playmates, instead preferring her own company as she hiked through the woods near her house. During these wanderings, she took to writing poetry, which she later set to music that she composed on her family's secondhand piano. A self-taught musician, Buffy began writing her own compositions at age four.

The tensions of her teenage years increased her shyness. She was ashamed of her olive skin and dark black hair and desperately wanted to be a blonde like the most popular girls in her high school. She was particularly uncomfortable at parties and other social gatherings. Describing this period of her life in *Ms.* magazine in 1975, Sainte-Marie said, "What was wrong with me? I used to ask myself. Now I know I simply felt bored, but then I blamed myself."

During this difficult time, Sainte-Marie retreated into her music. At 16, she discovered the guitar, which, like the piano, she taught herself to play. Free to experiment, she developed an assortment of unorthodox playing techniques; for instance, she created 32 different ways of tuning the guitar, each of which allowed her to create a unique type of sound.

In her midteens, Sainte-Marie also found comfort by exploring her heritage. Beginning by reading books about Indian history, she eventually searched out her Cree relatives, who warmly welcomed her back into the family. She later claimed that on her frequent visits to the Piapot Reserve as a teenager, she felt a far greater sense of security and community than she had known before.

In 1959, Sainte-Marie left home to study veterinary science at the University of Massachusetts. An excellent student, she soon changed her major to Eastern philosophy and education, with an eye toward a teaching career. While in college, Sainte-Marie also started singing her songs for her friends. They encouraged her to perform at coffeehouses in the area, which paid her $5 a night for entertaining their customers.

After graduating, Sainte-Marie considered traveling to India to continue her studies, but decided first to visit New York City and see if she could edge her way into the folk music scene there. For decades, Greenwich Village, a neighborhood in southern Manhattan, had been the home of several well-known nightclubs that showcased singers of traditional American folk songs. By the early 1960s, in response to the burgeoning popularity of folk music among college students, these clubs began featuring younger

singers who performed their own songs, many of which com-
mented on contemporary issues and events. The clubs recruited
most of their new talent through "hootenannies"—special shows
during which the mike was open to novice singer-songwriters
looking to build a following. By the time Sainte-Marie arrived in
Greenwich Village, several hootenanny veterans, such as Bob
Dylan, Joan Baez, and Peter, Paul, and Mary, had parlayed their
appearances into record contracts and national fame.

Sainte-Marie first began singing at Gerde's Folk City's Monday-
night hootenannies, where her performances earned Dylan's admiration. Partly through his influence, she made her debut at the
renowned Gaslight Cafe on August 17, 1963. In her audience that
night was Robert Sheldon, the music critic for the *New York Times.*
The next day, he announced in his column that he had just seen
"one of the most promising new talents on the folk scene."

Bolstered by many more rave reviews, Sainte-Marie quickly
attracted a legion of loyal fans, including some of the movers and
shakers of the entertainment industry. Among them were talent
scouts from Vanguard Records, the company that recorded many
of the most respected artists of the folk music boom. When Vanguard offered Sainte-Marie a contract, her first reaction was to run
from New York and the limelight. She retreated to a Maine
hideaway, where the reluctant star asked herself whether she
really wanted to work in show business. After several weeks of
soul-searching, she returned to the city, fully committed to pur-
suing a career as a professional singer.

In 1964, Vanguard released Sainte-Marie's first album, *It's My
Way.* A popular and critical success, the record gave her a national
audience and earned her the title "Best New Artist of the Year"
from *Billboard,* a trade magazine of the music industry. It also
established her as one of the label's biggest stars. For nearly a
decade, she would produce for Vanguard nearly an album a year,
most notably *Many a Mile* (1964), *Little Wheel Spin and Spin* (1966),
and *Illuminations* (1968).

With the reception of *It's My Way,* Sainte-Marie was flooded
with offers to appear at concerts throughout the United States and
Canada. By 1967, she had graduated from playing small clubs to

Buffy Sainte-Marie in the recording studio in the mid-1960s.
(UPI/Bettmann)

filling huge concert houses, such as Carnegie Hall and the New
York Philharmonic Hall. Sainte-Marie's reputation as a dynamic
performer attracted capacity crowds in even the largest theaters.
As a musician, she always surprised her audiences with her
distinctive ways of playing the guitar and with her usual selection
of instruments. Her concerts often featured a demonstration of the

mouthbow, a Native American instrument introduced to Sainte-Marie by Cree folk artist Patrick Sky. But most of her fans were drawn to her concerts by her unique singing style. In 1967, a reporter for the *New York News* aptly described her vocal talents:

> She sings in a clear, husky-timbred voice that can be sweet, low-down, bitter, compassionate, sprightly, sexy, or wryly humorous. She can purr or belt, warm you into a smile or near chill you with a trembling intensity.

In Sainte-Marie's own estimation, her greatest talent was as a songwriter. For her, the composing process was always exciting and unpredictable; a complete tune and set of lyrics often came to Sainte-Marie in a single flash of inspiration. As she explained in her 1975 *Ms.* interview: "I could be riding a taxi, an airplane, or eating. I don't have to be sad or happy to write. It can't be forced. A song is there all of a sudden, when it wasn't there before."

Throughout the 1960s, Sainte-Marie was one of the most prolific songwriters in the music business. Her songwriting range was also extraordinary. Her country tunes were performed by Chet Atkins and Dottie West; her works with a hard rock edge were covered by artists such as Janis Joplin; and her love songs were performed by nearly every popular singer of the day. Her most well-known love ballad of the era, "Until It's Time for You to Go" (1965), quickly became a standard. It has been recorded by hundreds of singers, including Bob Dylan, Barbra Streisand, Sonny and Cher, and Sainte-Marie's childhood idol, Elvis Presley.

As a performer, however, Sainte-Marie became most closely associated with the protest song. Like other folk artists, she used her music to comment on the politics of the day, particularly to denounce the United States's involvement in the Vietnam War. Sainte-Marie's greatest antiwar song was "Universal Soldier," which she first began singing in coffeehouses in 1963. Its lyrics recounted the horror of warfare throughout history and challenged listeners to confront their own responsibility, whether through direct support or inaction, in allowing their nation to engage in war. The message was deemed so controversial that Sainte-Marie was banned from singing "Universal Soldier" on radio or television for two years. The song became widely known only after it was covered by the popular rock artist Donovan in 1965. His version became a hit and helped make the song the unofficial anthem of the growing protest movement against the war in Vietnam.

Most of Sainte-Marie's protest songs dealt with the United States's treatment of Native Americans. Drawing on both her academic research into Indian history and her own observations of reservation life, she tried to enlighten her audiences about the U.S. government's historic theft of Indian land and the subsequent destruction of native ways of life. Among these songs were "Native American Child," "Now That the Buffalo's Gone," and "My Country 'Tis of Thy People You're Dying."

Sainte-Marie's outspokenness about Indian affairs soon led audiences and the media to type her as "the Indian folk singer," an image she resented, feeling that it prevented the public from seeing her as a multi-dimensional artist. In a profile in *Life* magazine in 1965, she reminded her listeners that, "I have written hundreds of songs and only a half dozen are of protest. I believe in leaving politics to the experts, only sometimes the experts don't know what's going on." In reality, Sainte-Marie took a far more active role in Indian causes than this comment suggested. At the height of her singing career, she spent much of her time touring reserves and reservations, where she gave lectures and performed benefit concerts. She also donated a sizable percentage of her earnings to several charities that aided Native American women and artists and to the Nihewan Foundation, an organization she established to provide law school scholarships to Indian students.

During the late 1960s, the American public's interest in folk music began to ebb. At the same time, Sainte-Marie's popularity in the United States started to wane, which she blamed, in part, to her reputation as a protest singer and activist. In Europe, Japan, and Australia, however, she remained a top draw throughout the 1970s. One of her foreign admirers, Queen Elizabeth II of England, recognized Sainte-Marie's contribution to international culture by awarding the singer a medal following a command performance she gave in Canada.

While Sainte-Marie's touring career flourished overseas, she grew so disappointed with the lackluster sales of her albums that she decided to leave Vanguard in 1973. She went on to record two albums for MCA and one for ABC Records, but neither company gave her work the publicity push she felt it deserved. In 1975, just months after ABC Records went out of business, Sainte-Marie gave birth to a son, whom she named Dakota. Her disillusionment with the music business and eagerness to be with her baby convinced her that the time was right to take a hiatus from recording.

Sainte-Marie continued to perform in Europe, but for the next decade in the United States she sang only on Indian reservations and at concerts to benefit UNICEF, the United Nations Children's Fund. However, she remained in the public eye by joining the cast of the children's television series "Sesame Street," on which she had first appeared in 1976. In the March 28, 1977 issue of *TV Guide*, she explained her mission on the show was to teach children that "Indians say more than 'ugh' and 'how.'" Sainte-Marie contributed several original songs to the program during her five-year tenure as a cast member.

Long interested in the medium of film, Sainte-Marie also began to experiment with several aspects of movie making. She scored two films, *Harold of Orange* (1986) and *Where the Spirit Lives* (1989), and narrated *Broken Rainbow* (1985), an Academy Award–winning documentary about the United States's treatment of the Navajo Indians. Five years earlier, Sainte-Marie had received her greatest nod from Hollywood for cowriting "Up Where We Belong." The song, which was featured on the soundtrack of the romantic drama *An Officer and a Gentleman*, won Sainte-Marie her own Oscar for Best Song in 1982.

Sainte-Marie also found time in the 1980s to return to the University of Massachusetts, where she earned a Ph.D. in Fine Arts. On her own, she explored another intellectual pursuit—educating herself about the latest advances in electronic and computer technology. Sainte-Marie recognized that by learning to use computers and synthesizers, she could create a home recording studio, where, acting as her own sound engineer, she could maintain complete control over the music she produced.

A publicity photograph of Sainte-Marie used to promote her acclaimed comeback album, Coincidence and Likely Stories (1992).   (Courtesy of EMI Records Group)

Impressed by one of her homemade tapes, Ensign Records coaxed Sainte-Marie out of her recording retirement to create *Coincidence and Likely Stories* (1992). The album's coproducer, she worked entirely from the studio she built in her house in Kauai, Hawaii. After singing her vocals directly into the recording equipment in her Macintosh computer, she laid down the instrumental tracks using synthesizers. The recordings then were sent to her fellow producer in London by modem. Sainte-Marie sees her work with computer technology as a logical extension of her years of musical experimentation. In a 1992 press release, she asserted, "Voice, mouthbow, guitar, computer . . . they're all just tools in the hands of artists."

Despite her new tools and new sound, many of the songs on *Coincidence and Likely Stories* harken back to her earlier work in their attacks on the world's "money and power junkies." For instance, "The Big Ones Get Away" comments on the moral lapses of government officials during the Iran-Contra scandal, and "The Priests of the Golden Bull" condemns the executives of the uranium mining companies whose greed has resulted in the destruction of reservation lands in the West. Sainte-Marie, however, strikes a completely different tone on "Starwalker." Featuring sounds recorded at an Indian powwow on the reserve on which she was born, the song is one of Sainte-Marie's most inspiring celebrations of Native American culture.

◆ ◆ ◆

While promoting *Coincidence and Likely Stories,* Buffy Sainte-Marie told a reporter from *Los Angeles* magazine that "regardless of what my career or my lyrics have been about, the record should be judged on only one thing: I either stand up to Mariah Carey and Bryan Adams or I've failed." Like many of her comments to the press, the statement seems intended to surprise and provoke its readers. Certainly her longtime fans would be appalled by the idea of holding up Sainte-Marie's personal, passionate, and intelligent songs to the standards set by most contemporary pop music.

Sainte-Marie, however, has always invited the comparison. Throughout her career, she has aimed to reach a mass audience, and in the 1960s, her political songs helped her achieve her goal. During that period, the era of the civil rights movement, Americans were reexamining their society's treatment of all minorities. As progressiveness in politics became more popular, minority performers, especially those who spoke out against the injustices of the past, became fashionable.

But like most cultural trends, this special interest in minority performers soon passed. In the 1970s, Sainte-Marie saw her popularity fading, largely because of the media attention her ethnic roots had previously drawn. As she explained in the *Los Angeles*

Times in 1978, "my fall was a matter of politics rather than mass listener turn-off."

As a prominent performer from a minority group, Sainte-Marie has run a risk throughout her career. To be honest with herself, she has felt compelled to use her art to discuss her ethnicity and its effect on her life, even though by doing so many people have typed her as a fringe artist with little to communicate to a larger audience. Her longevity in the music business, however, has helped to dispel this image. Remaining true to her artistic vision, her work has successfully survived social fashions and musical trends, all the while retaining a loyal following and attracting new, younger listeners along the way.

JOHN TRUDELL

◆ ◆ ◆

Santee Sioux Recording Artist
(1946–   )

"Sometimes they have to kill us because they can't break our spirit," explains Jimmy Looks Twice to the FBI agent who has been stalking him.

The agent, his confidence in his mission rapidly fading, wants to know more. He asks the fugitive why the government regards him and the other Indian activists of the Aboriginal Rights Movement as such a threat.

Speaking slowly and clearly, Jimmy tells him, "We choose the right to be who we are. We know the difference between the reality of freedom and the illusion of freedom." He pauses to light a pipe handed to him by an elder, a respected holy man, then, in a phrase, reveals the simple truth that the agent has not been able to grasp: "It's about power, Ray."

In this pivotal scene from the 1992 movie *Thunderheart*, John Trudell, who plays Jimmy, delivers a riveting and chilling performance, cited by many reviewers as the film's highlight. The assurance Trudell displays in the part—his first in a major motion picture—reveals not only natural talent, but also an intimate knowledge of his character. To a large degree, Jimmy was based on Trudell and his role as the chairman of the American Indian Movement, the organization on which the Aboriginal Rights

In Thunderheart (1992), *Trudell (right) was featured in the role of an Indian activist, a character that was in part modeled on his own experiences in the 1970s.* (Courtesy of the Museum of Modern Art Film Stills Archive)

Movement was modeled. In his portrayal, Trudell draws on the skills he developed as an activist in the 1970s and continues to hone as a recording artist today—the ability to move listeners with powerful words, powerfully spoken.

◆ ◆ ◆

Born in Omaha, Nebraska, on February 15, 1946, John Trudell grew up on and near the Santee Sioux Indian Reservation, a small tract resting on the border between South Dakota and Nebraska. Until the 1860s, the Santees had lived in present-day Minnesota. After waging a bloody and unsuccessful uprising against the white settlers who had invaded their territory, the tribe had to flee their homeland and seek refuge with their Teton Sioux relatives to the south. In Teton territory, they found little relief from warfare, however. There, skirmishes between the Sioux and their white neighbors continued until 1890, the year of the Wounded Knee M assacre. This incident, in which more than 150 Sioux men, women, and children were slaughtered by the U.S. Army, marked the end of the Sioux's military resistance to white encroachment of their lands.

During his youth, Trudell saw firsthand the legacy of the Sioux's defeat in the Plains Wars. More than a half century of confinement on reservations had destroyed the Indians' traditional economy and culture. In their place, the Sioux were left with rampant unemployment, inadequate housing and health care, and few educational opportunities. By the time of Trudell's birth, reservation Indians had become the poorest minority in the United States.

Eager to escape the poverty and hopelessness of the reservation, Trudell enlisted in the U.S. Navy when he turned 17. He spent most of his four-year tour of duty aboard a ship stationed off the coast of Vietnam. Although Trudell did not engage in any active combat during the Vietnam War, his experiences in the country left him shaken. He was shocked and disgusted both with the military's systematic discrimination against him and other minority troops and with the racist attitudes many American soldiers displayed toward the Asian civilians they had been sent overseas supposedly to protect.

Disillusioned and aimless, Trudell returned to the United States in 1967. During the next two years, he worked odd jobs while drifting in and out of college. His life began to take on direction only after he joined the Indians of All Tribes in 1969. This organization was one of several formed in the late 1960s by young Native Americans who, like Trudell, were enraged by the U.S. government's unjust treatment of Indian people and the dismal living conditions on most reservations. They looked for guidance and inspiration not from the government-supported tribal councils that officially governed reservations, but from Indian elders who tried to keep their people's ancient traditions alive.

To draw attention to their grievances, the Indians of All Tribes staged a dramatic protest. In 1969, the group took control of Alcatraz, a small island off the coast of San Francisco, California, that had once housed a maximum security federal prison. The activists had little practical use for Alcatraz; the takeover was primarily a symbolic act intended to shed light on the U.S. government's historical seizure of Indian land.

A small faction of the Indians of All Tribes occupied Alcatraz for 19 months before they were ousted by U.S. troops. Although the Alcatraz takeover had little immediate impact on federal policy, the extensive media coverage of the event did succeed in bringing the group's cause before the American public. The takeover also provided John Trudell with an outlet for his energy and intelligence. A gifted orator, he emerged as the group's primary spokesman during the long protest.

Beginning in 1973, Trudell put his newfound talents to use as the national chairman for the American Indian Movement (AIM), an activist group founded in Minneapolis, Minnesota, in 1968. AIM had gained nationwide notoriety through a 71-day occupation of the site of the 1890 Wounded Knee Massacre on the Pine Ridge Indian Reservation in South Dakota. Largely as a result of the protest at Wounded Knee, the FBI regarded AIM leaders as enemies of the government and held them under close surveillance. The agency's thorough scrutiny of Trudell and his activities in the 1970s resulted in a 17,000-page file, which was made public in 1986 through the Freedom of Information Act. The FBI file described Trudell as "an intelligent individual and eloquent speaker who has the ability to stimulate people into action. . . . In short, he is an extremely effective agitator."

Trudell was particularly eloquent in his defense of Leonard Peltier, an AIM activist charged with the murder of two FBI agents on Pine Ridge in 1975. After publicly accusing the FBI of framing Peltier during his trial, Trudell was banned from the courtroom and sentenced to six months in prison for contempt of court. In jail, a fellow inmate told Trudell that his family might get hurt if he continued to speak out—a warning that he later insisted that the FBI had instructed the prison messenger to pass along.

On February 11, 1979, at a demonstration outside the FBI headquarters in Washington, D.C., Trudell flagrantly ignored the advice. During the protest, he denounced the agency and burned an American flag. Less than 12 hours later, another fire erupted thousands of miles away on the Shoshone-Paiute Indian

Reservation in Nevada. The blaze destroyed the house of Trudell's father-in-law and took the lives of Trudell's wife Tina, their three preschool-age children, and his mother-in-law. Following a cursory investigation, the FBI and the Bureau of Indian Affairs declared that the fire was a tragic accident. Trudell, however, remains convinced that his family was murdered by his political adversaries.

After the death of his wife and children, Trudell resigned from AIM for fear that other relatives and friends might be killed if he continued his work with the organization. Consumed by grief, he spent the next six months in a deep depression. As he explained to a *New York Times* reporter in 1992, "I just wandered, I knew that I was moving into madness, and I didn't know how long that drift was going to last, or if I just rode it, maybe I could survive. I considered that my time of exile." Remembering his late wife's love of writing poetry finally helped Trudell emerge from this dark period. As a form of therapy, he began composing his own poems, a creative release that he now claims saved his life. According to Trudell, "the lines were my bombs, my explosions, my tears, they were my everything."

In the early 1980s, Trudell once again started making public appearances at political rallies, where he lent his support to antinuclear and environmental causes. Through this work, he met singer-activist Jackson Browne, who encouraged Trudell to set his poetry to music. Trudell's first attempts resulted in an unreleased recording entitled *Tribal Voice*, on which he read a few of his poems to an accompaniment of traditional Indian chants and drumming.

Unsatisfied with the sound of *Tribal Voice*, Trudell next tried a completely different approach. Working with Jesse Ed Davis, a noted rock guitarist and member of the Kiowa tribe, he began mixing his spoken word recordings with blues-rock rhythms created with electric guitars, synthesizers, and drum machines. Calling themselves the Grafitti Band, Trudell and Davis recorded their first album, *AKA Grafitti Man*, in 1986 on Trudell's own label. Initially, the record was sold only through mail order and at the band's shows. But demand grew when rock star Bob Dylan called it "the best album of 1986" in *Rolling Stone* magazine and began playing it over the PA system during intermissions at his concerts.

Trudell and Davis continued their collaboration until Davis's death in 1988, after which Grafitti Band guitarist Mark Shark began providing the music for Trudell's song-poems. In 1992, the independent label Rykodisc Records released an album of the best tracks produced by Trudell with Davis and Shark over the previous six years. Also titled *AKA Grafitti Man*, the recording was a great critical success, praised both for its style and substance. Many reviewers favorably compared Trudell's cool, clear, sometimes hypnotic reading of his poems to the vocal delivery of rock legend Lou Reed. Trudell was also hailed for his range as a writer. Among the songs on *AKA Grafitti Man* are "Rockin' the Res," a celebration of the spiritual strength of Indian communities; "Bombs Over Baghdad," a stinging indictment of the United States's involvement in the Persian Gulf War; and "Baby Boom Ché," an affectionate homage to Elvis Presley and his impact on Trudell's generation.

Within months of the release of *AKA Grafitti Man*, Trudell made his motion picture debut in two films. In *Incident at Oglala*, a documentary directed by Michael Apted that chronicles the 1975 Pine Ridge shootings and the Peltier trial, he is interviewed at length. Displaying the articulateness and intensity that had made him AIM's leading spokesperson, he vividly describes the escalating atmosphere of hostility between the FBI and the reservation residents before and after the murders. Impressed by Trudell's screen presence, Apted asked him to try his hand at acting in *Thunderheart*, the director's fictionalized account of events on Pine Ridge during the 1970s. In the eyes of several reviewers, Trudell stole the movie with his performance as activist Jimmy Looks Twice, a character that amalgamates aspects of his and Peltier's personalities and experiences.

According to Trudell, he initially accepted the small role because he was intrigued by the idea of speaking scripted lines. During the filming, however, he balked at reading the dialogue he was given, which he felt did not realistically depict the sentiments of his character. At Apted's urging, Trudell rewrote most of his scenes.

After the filming was complete, Trudell toured the United States as a featured performer in the 1993 WOMAD (World of Music, Art, and Dance) Festival—an annual celebration of world music featuring performers from more than twenty countries around the globe. He then returned to the recording studio and in 1994 released his second album with Rykodisc, *Johnny Damas and Me,* on which he experimented further with combining traditional Indian music with rock and blues instrumentation. In an interview with *Billboard* magazine, Trudell observed that with the album he was "trying to achieve a genuine fusion, not use contemporary music to imitate traditional music or vice versa."

Like *AKA Grafitti Man, Johnny Damas and Me* has won critical acclaim for its breadth of subject matter. On tracks, such as "Shadow Over Sisterland" and "Baby Doll Blues," Trudell explores the treatment of women in American society, particularly the gulf between the dreams of girlhood and the harsh realities adult women must face. He also includes several love songs, such as "Something About You" and "After All These Years," the latter a tribute to the memory of his late wife. But perhaps the album's most personal song is "Rant n Roll," a hard-driving anthem that dares the listener to "say what you mean." The title alone effectively and succinctly sums up Trudell's goals as a performer—to meld the activist's voice with a rock 'n' roll sensibility.

◆ ◆ ◆

Despite his glowing reviews and growing popular following, John Trudell is not without his critics. Some Native Americans have maintained that Trudell's career as a recording artist amounts to a betrayal of the ideals he articulated so effectively as AIM's chairman. These detractors accuse Trudell of abandoning his commitment to politics to become a rock star.

By Trudell's own admission, touring with a band is a far more comfortable way of life than battling the FBI. But at the root, the goals of Trudell's work as a performer are little different than those he had as an activist. As he explained in *Billboard* magazine in January 1994, "I'm not really trying to entertain *or* deliver a message. I'm trying to communicate." It was just this desire to

This photograph, used to publicize his 1994 album Johnny Damas and Me, *captures John Trudell's subdued appearance and controlled demeanor during his concert performances.* (Courtesy of Rykodisc Records)

communicate that made the FBI regard Trudell as a threat in the 1970s. As the agency's records indicate, Trudell was considered dangerous to the public good not because of a tendency toward violence, but because of his facility with words and his charisma as a speaker.

Trudell no longer belongs to any political organization. His experiences with AIM have made him suspicious of politics in general, which he maintains encourages competition rather than cooperation between people and groups. Today, he instead puts his faith in art and in its ability to explore and expose basic truths. As he explained in *Spin* magazine in August 1992:

> All I can do is put forth truth in my words and hope they make a small impact on the listeners' psyches. If nothing else, I can go to bed at night knowing I've stood up to the lies and hypocrisy in my own little way.

GRAHAM GREENE

◆ ◆ ◆

Oneida Stage and Film Actor
(1952–   )

Circled around a tipi fire, the men of the camp have gathered to discuss the latest threat to their homeland. Tired of talk, Wind in His Hair, the most respected of the young warriors, stands up and declares that their worries are foolish. The man living alone in the old fort is not a Sioux, but one of the whites. Like the others, he cannot ride a horse or shoot a rifle. He is not worthy of their respect or concern. Wind in His Hair insists that they should kill the white stranger and forget him.

The warriors laugh and murmur their agreement, until one man, a quiet presence among the group, raises his hand to show that he wants to speak. The gesture silences the young men, who all turn their attention toward Kicking Bird, eager to hear his opinion. In a calm voice, he says that he agrees with Wind in His Hair; the whites are a poor race, but they are not as harmless as his young friend allows. Many more whites will be coming to their lands, Kicking Bird explains. He reasons that the Sioux must make an effort to speak to this white man as a first step toward forging a peace with the others who are sure to follow.

Just as Kicking Bear captivates his audience in this scene, Graham Greene, the actor who played the character in the historical epic *Dances With Wolves* (1990), entranced American moviegoers

Graham Greene as Kicking Bird in Dances With Wolves, *the role that earned him an Academy Award nomination for Best Supporting Actor of 1990.* (Courtesy of the Museum of Modern Art Film Stills Archive)

with his composed performance. Credited with atoning for Hollywood's long history of stereotyping Indians as savages with its sympathetic portrayal of the Teton Sioux, the movie became an international hit, a critical success, and the winner of the 1990 Academy Award for Best Picture. Greene's contribution to the film was acknowledged with an Oscar nomination for Best

Supporting Actor. Following the trail blazed by Chief Dan George, who was nominated for his performance in *Little Big Man* (1970), Greene became the second Native American actor in film history to be so honored.

◆ ◆ ◆

Born in 1952, Graham Greene was reared on the Six Nations Reserve in Brantford, Ontario. His parents, John and Lillian Greene, were members of the Oneida Nation, one of the six tribes of the Iroquois Confederacy, but neither attempted to teach Graham and his five brothers and sisters about their heritage. According to Greene, his mother and father had been deeply affected by their experiences as students at government-run Indian boarding schools. Remembering well the beatings Indian girls and boys received for speaking their own language in these institutions, the Greenes were reluctant to share their knowledge of Oneida culture with their children.

Greene's memories of his own childhood are far more pleasant. In awe of the natural wonders of the reserve, he spent winters ice skating on frozen creeks and summers hiking through the forests. School, however, held much less fascination for him. Bored with his classes and wanting to set out on his own, Greene dropped out at 16 and left home to seek his fortune in the city.

His first stop was Rochester, New York, where he took a job in a carpet warehouse, but soon he returned to Canada, settling for a time in the town of Hamilton, Ontario. For several years, Greene worked at various factories before friends steered him to odd jobs in the music business in the early 1970s. After working as a roadie and a sound engineer, he eventually began operating his own recording studio in the town of Ancaster.

In 1974, an acquaintance asked Greene to act in a production of the Ne'er-Do-Well Thespians, a theater company in Toronto. The role was small, but the experience left him eager to give up his career in music for one in the theater. In a 1991 profile in *Maclean's* magazine, he described, with characteristic wit, the thought process behind his decision to devote himself to acting: "You dress up in funny clothes, stand around in bright lights and tell lies. . . .

No whining musicians to deal with—I can be a whiny actor. I thought that was fabulous."

For the next 17 years, Greene appeared in productions staged in small theaters throughout Canada. Acting in many contemporary Canadian plays, he portrayed a number of Native American characters. Among his most powerful performances was his depiction of an Indian alcoholic in the 1980 production of *The Crackwalker*.

By taking the part, Greene invited harsh criticism from the Indian community. Because of the historic prevalence of alcoholism among Native American populations, some Indians resist any depiction of the problem in the media for fear of promoting the centuries-old stereotype of Indians as heavy drinkers. Disregarding their cautions, Greene took the role with enthusiasm. At the time, he was a member of Alcoholics Anonymous, having survived his own trials with alcohol abuse in the 1970s. In his 1991 *Maclean's* profile, Greene explained his willingness to play an alcoholic character with the statement, "Before the healing can take place, the poison must first be exposed."

By the early 1980s, Greene began to find work in movies in Canada and the United States. He had small roles in *Running Brave* (1983), a portrait of Sioux Indian track star Billy Mills, and *Revolution* (1985), a hugely expensive epic about the American Revolutionary War that failed to find an audience at the box office. However, his burgeoning film career was halted by the 1984 death of his father. Deeply affected by his loss, Greene briefly abandoned acting and moved to the country, determined to make his living off the land.

In the end, however, Greene's attraction to the city and the theater proved too great. He soon returned to Toronto, where he appeared in *The History of the Village of the Small Huts*, a series of surreal plays that recount Canadian history, at the Theatre Passe Muraille. Aside from taking a small role in *Powwow Highway* (1989), a well-received drama about contemporary Indian life, Greene devoted his time and talents to the fledgling company, to which he offered his services welding sets and working lights when he was not on stage. The rewards for his hard work and long hours at the theater were purely creative. By the late 1980s, the struggling actor's only income came from selling hand-painted T-shirts on the street.

In 1989, Greene's life changed dramatically when he was cast for a leading role in *Dances With Wolves*, a western about a U.S. soldier's experiences among the Teton Sioux in the 1860s. After viewing Greene's audition tape, Kevin Costner—the movie's co-producer, director, and star—initially was hesitant to hire Greene because of his appearance. As Costner explained in his 1990 book about the movie, "[Greene] doesn't come off right away as a strong Indian 'type,' so at first I saw just the professional actor rather than some sculpted guy that maybe I was looking for." Finding the part extremely difficult to cast, Costner took a second look and this time saw how well Greene's "low-key style fit the character."

In *Dances*, Greene appeared as Kicking Bear, a holy man who befriends John Dunbar, the soldier portrayed by Costner. Screenwriter Michael Blake based Greene's character on the historical Kicking Bear, a Kiowa chief who led his tribe's peace faction during the Plains Wars. An advocate for the peaceful coexistence of Indians and whites, Kicking Bear died in 1875, possibly poisoned by a member of the Kiowa's militant faction that sought to remove non-Indians from their lands by force.

Like the actual Kicking Bear, Greene's character is his tribe's moral center. He encourages his people to attempt to communicate with Dunbar, a gesture that endears the Sioux to the soldier. In part because of his friendship with Kicking Bear, Dunbar eventually decides to renounce white society and become a member of the tribe.

For Greene, the filming of *Dances* was an education. To prepare for the role, he studied Teton Sioux history and culture and was tutored in the tribe's language, which he spoke on screen in many of his scenes. As a result of his research, Greene soon knew more about the Sioux than about his own people. Disturbed by his ignorance of Oneida culture, he was inspired to explore his roots.

After receiving fine reviews and an Oscar nomination for his work in *Dances*, Greene was deluged with movie offers. The majority were for films about Native Americans, who, because of

In the 1992 film Thunderheart, *Greene played a tribal policeman whose intelligence and wit helps solve the mystery behind a murder on a Sioux Indian reservation.* (Courtesy of the Museum of Modern Art Film Stills Archive)

Dances's success, suddenly had become a hot subject in Hollywood. From these many projects, Greene first chose a starring role in *Thunderheart* (1992), a fictionalized version of events that occurred on the Pine Ridge Indian Reservation in South Dakota during the 1970s. In the film, Greene plays Walter Crow Horse, a tribal policeman who is investigating the murder of a reservation resident. Reluctantly, he finds himself working alongside a young FBI agent, Raymond Levoi (Val Kilmer), who has been chosen for the assignment because he is part Indian. As in *Dances,* Greene's character instructs the stranger about the ways of the Sioux and, in the process, turns his adversary into his friend. Like John Dunbar, Raymond Levoi in the end chooses to join the Sioux in their battles against government authorities.

Also in 1992, Greene appeared in *Clearcut,* a Canadian film about a young Indian activist named Arthur who kidnaps the manager of a lumber mill when its workers desecrate his tribe's sacred grounds. After the filming was complete, Greene publicly criticized the violent psychological thriller. Nevertheless, many reviewers singled out his charismatic performance as Arthur—a character whose comic energy and supernatural power recalls the trickster hero of many Indian legends. A *New York Times* review described Greene's Arthur as radiating "the glamour of a survivalist who is so perfectly attuned to nature that he moves through the wilderness with the confidence of a god."

In addition to his film work, Greene has taken on many television roles. He has appeared as a guest star on several series, playing, for instance, a Navajo lawyer on "L.A. Law" and a Native American healer on "Northern Exposure." Greene has also acted in several television movies, including "Cooperstown" (1993) and "The Last of His Tribe" (1992), which Greene identifies as one of his favorite projects.

Based on actual events, "The Last of His Tribe" depicts the story of Ishi, the only Yahi Indian to survive the slaughter of his tribe by white settlers and prospectors in the late 19th century. Taken in by anthropologist Albert Kroeber (Jon Voight), Ishi gradually learns the English language and the manners and customs of whites. Kroeber in turn becomes Ishi's student, learning not only about the Yahis' history and culture but also from the Indian's respect and reverence for the natural world.

◆ ◆ ◆

In a 1992 solicitation letter for the American Indian College Fund, Graham Greene identified a common thread linking the various roles he has played in films and on television: "I have often portrayed Native people who serve as spiritual leaders. Whether the action took place in the 1700s, the early 1900s, or the 1970s, the Native character that I have played helped someone else—usually the white man—see." As Greene's comment suggests, Hollywood at last has begun to treat Native American actors with the respect they have long deserved. Throughout most of film history, Indian actors and actresses had been offered only a tiny range of roles— usually fierce warriors, stoic war leaders, lovelorn maidens, or exotic seductresses. Even worse, in most of these parts, their people have been depicted as evil or ignorant, thus encouraging the audience either to despise Indians for their immorality or to pity them for their inferiority.

Because of changes in the public's view of Native Americans, Greene has had the chance to play a wealth of parts that champion Native Americans and celebrate their cultures. But, to some extent, he too has suffered from typecasting. Again and again, he has been asked to portray a new Indian "type"—the noble wise man who becomes a non-Indian's moral teacher. Although such roles certainly present Indians in a positive light, they often fail to show Native Americans as fully rounded people. Also in these parts, Indians frequently are used only as catalysts for the spiritual growth of non-Indians, rather than treated as interesting characters in their own right.

The entertainment industry has succeeded in discarding most of the Indian stereotypes it once promoted. But today it faces a new test. Hollywood must now rise to the challenge posed by Graham Greene and other skilled Native American actors to create roles for them that are equal to their considerable talents.

SELECTED
ANNOTATED BIBLIOGRAPHY
AND FURTHER READING

◆ ◆ ◆

Emily Pauline Johnson

Johnson, E. Pauline. *The Moccasin Maker.* Tucson: University of Arizona Press, 1987. Reprint of a collection of Johnson's stories and articles originally published in *Mother's Magazine.* The informative introduction by A. LaVonne Brown Ruoff discusses Johnson's unique treatment of female Indian characters and compares her work with that of other women writers of her day.

————. *Flint and Feather.* Toronto: Hodder & Stoughton, 1912. Compilation of Johnson's poetry, including her earlier collections, *The White Wampum* and *Canadian Born.*

Keller, Betty. *Pauline: A Biography of Pauline Johnson.* Vancouver: Douglas & McIntyre, 1981. This definitive biography of Johnson provides a detailed account of her life, especially of her early years and their influence on her career.

Shrive, Norman. "What Happened to Pauline?" *Canadian Literature,* vol. 12, Summer 1962, pp. 25–38. A balanced reassessment of Johnson's importance in Canadian literary history.

Van Stern, Marcus. *Pauline Johnson: Her Life and Work.* Toronto: Hodder & Stoughton, 1965. A brief and highly laudatory biography of Johnson with selections of her best-known poetry and prose.

Luther Standing Bear

The Brooklyn Museum. *Buffalo Bill and the Wild West.* Brooklyn: The Brooklyn Museum, 1981. A well-illustrated collection of articles on various aspects of Buffalo Bill's Wild West Show. Of particular interest is an examination of the Indians' role in the show written by Lakota Sioux writer and activist Vine Deloria.

Ellis, Richard N. "Luther Standing Bear." In *Indian Lives: Essays on Nineteenth- and Twentieth-Century Native American Leaders,* edited by L. G. Moses and Raymond Wilson, pp. 139–158. Albuquerque: University of New Mexico Press, 1985. A brief essay that discusses Standing Bear's life, career, and influence.

Standing Bear, Luther. *My People, the Sioux,* reprint. Lincoln: University of Nebraska Press, 1975. This memoir, originally published in 1928, concentrates on Standing Bear's experiences among non-Indians and includes a chapter about his 1902 tour with Buffalo Bill's Wild West Show.

———. *Land of the Spotted Eagle,* reprint. Lincoln: University of Nebraska Press, 1978. Standing Bear's 1934 examination of the traditions of the Teton Sioux and condemnation of their treatment by non-Indians and the U.S. government.

———. *My Indian Boyhood,* reprint. Lincoln: University of Nebraska Press, 1988. An account of Standing Bear's childhood, which he wrote for non-Indian children in 1931.

Will Rogers

Brown, William R. *Imagemaker: Will Rogers and the American Dream.* Columbia: University of Missouri Press, 1970. A dense but illuminating discussion of Rogers's role as an American hero. May be too difficult for young readers.

Gibson, Arrell Morgan, ed. *Will Rogers: A Centennial Tribute.* Oklahoma City: Oklahoma Historical Society, 1979. Essays by nine scholars on Rogers's career and influence.

Ketchum, Richard M. *Will Rogers: The Man and His Times.* New York: American Heritage Publishing Company, 1973. This lively biography includes an excellent selection of photographs and memorabilia from the Will Rogers Memorial.

Sterling, Bryan B., and Frances B. Sterling, eds. *A Will Rogers Treasury: Reflections and Observations.* New York: Crown Publishers, 1982. A chronologically arranged compilation of Rogers's newspaper columns published between 1922 and 1935.

Yagoda, Ben. *Will Rogers.* New York: Alfred A. Knopf, 1993. The most recent and definitive published account of Rogers's life.

Iron Eyes Cody

Books

Bataille, Gretchen M, ed. *The Pretend Indians.* Ames, IA: Iowa University Press, 1980. A collection of scholarly essays about Indians and the film industry. May be too difficult for young readers.

British Film Institute. *The BFI Companion to the Western.* New York: Atheneum, 1988. This encyclopedia of films, filmmakers, and actors includes a brief, thorough history of American westerns and the portrayal of Indians in them.

Cody, Iron Eyes, and Collin Perry. *Iron Eyes: My Life as a Hollywood Indian.* New York: Everest House, 1982. Cody's chatty, "as-told-to" autobiography offers his insights into his career and the evolution of Indian characters on film.

Films

Blaustein, Julian, producer. *Broken Arrow.* Livonia, MI: Key Video. Videotape, 93 min., 1988. The 1950 western classic starring Jeff Chandler, James Stewart, and Jay Silverheels features Cody in one of his first notable roles.

Howard, Sandy, producer. *A Man Called Horse.* Farmington Hills, MI: CBS/Fox Video. Videotape, 115 min., 1985. Cody appears as the medicine man in this 1970 film, which tells the story of a white man taken captive by the Sioux in 1820.

Maria Tallchief

Books and Articles

Mason, Frances, ed. *I Remember Balanchine: Recollections of the Ballet Master by Those Who Knew Him.* New York: Doubleday & Co., 1991. The chapter on Maria Tallchief is an extended interview, in which she describes her early years as a dancer and her relationship with Balanchine.

Maynard, Olga. *Bird of Fire: The Story of Maria Tallchief.* New York: Dodd, Mead, & Company, 1961. A biography that deals with Tallchief's career up to 1960.

Rautbord, Sugar. "Maria Tallchief." *Interview* 17, March 1987, pp. 60–63. A brief interview in which Tallchief reevaluates her career as a dancer, teacher, and company director.

Films

Belle, Anne, producer. "Dancing for Mr. B: Six Balanchine Ballerinas." Los Angeles: Direct Cinema, Ltd. Videotape, 94 min., 1989. A documentary originally aired as part of the PBS series *Dance in America.* The program features an interview with Tallchief and archival footage of her performances in *Firebird, Scotch Symphony,* and *Don Quixote.*

Buffy Sainte-Marie

Books and Articles

Braudy, Susan. "Buffy Sainte-Marie: 'Native North American Me.'" *Ms.,* vol. 4, March 1975, pp. 14–18. A lively midcareer profile, in which Sainte-Marie reflects on her early success.

Sainte-Marie, Buffy. *The Buffy Sainte-Marie Songbook.* New York: Grosset and Dunlop, 1971. In this compilation of her most popular compositions from the 1960s, Sainte-Marie discusses her theory of songwriting and the story behind many of her songs.

Turbide, Diane. "Songs that Sear." *Maclean's*, vol. 105, April 20, 1992, p. 53. In this brief interview, Sainte-Marie discusses her return to recording and her album *Coincidence and Likely Stories*.

Recordings

Sainte-Marie, Buffy. *It's My Way*. New York: Vanguard Records, 1964. Sainte-Marie's debut album, which includes her version of "Universal Soldier."

———. *The Best of Buffy Sainte-Marie, Vol. 1* and *Vol. 2*, Santa Monica: Vanguard Records, 1971. These two albums collect more than 40 of Sainte-Marie's most popular songs from the 1960s.

———. *Coincidence and Likely Stories*. Los Angeles: Ensign Records, 1992. Sainte-Marie's first album after a 14-year hiatus from recording. It includes several songs dealing with Indian issues, such as "Bury My Heart at Wounded Knee," "The Priests of the Golden Bull," and "Starwalker."

John Trudell

Books and Articles

Baird, Robert. "Taking Aim." *New Times* 23, June 17–23, 1992, pp. 90–91. An interview with Trudell in which he discusses the goals of his work and his opinions on politics.

Matthiessen, Peter. *In the Spirit of Crazy Horse*. New York: Viking Press, 1983. This is a detailed and disturbing account of the conflicts on the Pine Ridge Indian Reservation in the 1970s. It provides a history of the American Indian Movement and discusses Trudell's role as national chairman of the organization.

Tannenbaum, Rob. "The Man in Black." *Village Voice* 37, July 28, 1992, p. 69. A brief assessment of Trudell's political and recording career.

Films

Chobanian, Arthur, producer. *Incident at Oglala*. Van Nuys, CA: Live Home Video. Videotape, 90 min., 1991. This documentary about the Leonard Peltier case features an extensive interview with Trudell.

DeNiro, Robert, Jane Rosenthal, and John Fusco, producers. *Thunderheart.* Burbank, CA: Columbia Tristar Home Video. Videotape, 118 min., 1992. Trudell is featured in a small role as an activist leader in this fictionalized account of the conflicts between the FBI and AIM members.

Recordings

Trudell, John. *AKA Grafitti Man.* Salem, MA: Rykodisc Records, 1992. A remix of selected song-poems recorded by Trudell between 1986 and 1991.

———. *Johnny Damas and Me.* Salem, MA: Rykodisc Records, 1994. Trudell's second major release features traditional Indian chants and music on several of its 12 tracks.

Graham Greene

Books and Articles

Costner, Kevin, Michael Blake, and Jim Wilson. *Dances With Wolves: The Illustrated Story of the Epic Film.* New York: Newmarket Press, 1990. Heavily illustrated with movie stills, this book includes commentary from Greene and other cast members about their thoughts and experiences during filming.

Johnson, Brian D. "Dances With Oscar: Canadian Actor Graham Greene Tastes Stardom." *Maclean's* 104, March 25, 1991, pp. 50–51. An interview with Greene in which the actor describes his childhood and theater career.

Films

Wilson, Jim, and Kevin Costner, producers. *Dances With Wolves.* New York: Orion Home Video. Videotape, 181 min., 1991. The 1990 winner of the Academy Award for Best Picture, this film features Greene in a starring role as Kicking Bird, a Teton Sioux holy man, who advocates making peace with the whites who arrive in the tribe's territory in the 1860s.

DeNiro, Robert, Jane Rosenthal, and John Fusco. producers. *Thunderheart*. Burbank, CA: Columbia Tristar Home Video. Videotape, 118 min., 1992. Greene costars in this fictional retelling of the Teton Sioux's battles with the FBI on the Pine Ridge Indian Reservation in the 1970s. Greene plays a tribal policeman, who helps solve the mystery of an Indian man's murder despite the best efforts of the FBI to conceal the truth.

Wieringa, Jan. producer. *Powwow Highway*. Los Angeles: Cannon Video. Videotape, 91 min., 1989. This witty film about two Northern Cheyenne men—one a dreamer (Gary Farmer), one a realist (A Martinez)—dramatizes contemporary Indians' struggle to reconcile ancient beliefs with the harsh conditions of modern reservation life. In a brief scene, Greene delivers a powerful performance as a physically and emotionally scarred Vietnam veteran.

INDEX

Boldface numbers indicate main headings.
Italic numbers indicate illustrations.